The Historic

ARTUR, GWENWHYVAWR AND MYRDDIN

ANCIENT BRYTHONS OF THE NORTH

The Historic

ARTUR, GWENWHYVAWR AND MYRDDIN

ANCIENT BRYTHONS OF THE NORTH

Alexander and William McCall

First published in 1997 by
The Pentland Press Ltd.
1 Hutton Close
South Church
Bishop Auckland
Durham

British Library Cataloguing in Publication Data.
A catalogue record for this book is available
from the British Library.

ISBN 1 85821 489 0

Typeset by George Wishart, Whitley Bay.
Printed and bound by Antony Rowe Ltd, Chippenham.

This book is dedicated to our long suffering wives,
families and friends, who have for years put up
with a never ending diatribe on Ancient Britons with
strange sounding names and the unpronounceable
Irish Gaelic names of the Iro-Scots. To them all,
we extend our thanks.

ACKNOWLEDGEMENTS

Special thanks to Pauline Ludgate for secretarial work, map drawing and printing, and much other helping handiwork.

To Dr John Bannerman, Senior Lecturer in Scottish History, at the School of Scottish History, Edinburgh University, and author of *Studies in the History of Dalriada*, who unstintingly always answered our queries with good grace and enthusiasm, with what must have seemed to him, at times, requests from armchair historians.

To Professor Rick Lathe of the Centre for Genome Research and Neuroscience, Edinburgh University, and his wife Maggie, for reading the typescript and making invaluable suggestions to improve its appeal, hopefully, to publishers, who in general are wary of the possibility of an Artur or Arthur being of an early Brito-Scottish descent.

To the librarians of Loanhead Library, Midlothian, for their efforts in getting difficult to come-by books on our behalf.

To all our grateful thanks.

CONTENTS

ILLUSTRATIONS

ILLUSTRATIONS

FOREWORD

This book, is, one must suppose, lucky ever to have been written, since it is the endeavour of two brothers some fourteen years apart in age, which meant the elder working and living mostly in England, while the younger spent most of his life a native of Scotland. This resulted in very little contact between them, and so little knowledge of each other's interests.

This condition lasted for many years, until their father, now a widower, came to live out the rest of his life with the younger brother; this meant much more contact, including visits, by Alex, his father's namesake.

It was on one such visit that some remarks were made about early Scottish history, particularly in what was known as the Dark Ages, and it came to light that both had a similar interest, Alex, the elder, in the early history of the Lordship of the Isles, and William, the younger, in the early Britons of Southern Scotland, known as the Gwyr Y Gogled or 'Men of the North'. They then both realised that the periods being studied covered the time of a person called 'King Arthur'.

They exchanged many heated views on the subject of Arthur. Alex claimed him to be Artur son of Aidan Mac Gabhran, and William thought him to be either Artrwys son of Mar or Urien of Rheged. William decided to bring things to a head by writing down the pros and cons of the various arguments. This decided, he got to thirty-six arguments in favour of his elder brother's views, and decided that was enough on that side of the question and it was now time to get on with his 'Cons' and wipe the floor with his adversary. To his great dismay he could not come up with any more than some eight or so arguments for his stance.

This shattering experience to his ego was difficult enough to accept, but to have to ring his elder brother, admitting defeat, and swing himself behind, a concept new to him, was a little disquieting to say the least.

However, once having bitten the bullet, it has been a rewarding experience, each learning much from the other's historical point of view. So much so that a few years ago, a decision was made to see if we could make a book of it. Unfortunately ill health on both our parts, over the last three years, has delayed the final completion until now. We hope it will be an enjoyable and thought-provoking read.

ALEXANDER MCCALL,   WILLIAM S. MCCALL,
BROCKTON,   ROSLIN,
SHROPSHIRE,   MIDLOTHIAN,
ENGLAND.   SCOTLAND.
1997.   1997.

INTRODUCTION

The mythology that has grown up around 'King' Arthur and his consort 'Queen' Gwenevere, his court 'magician' Merlin and his many 'Knights of the Round Table', has always provoked the question, are they based on real historic people?

This problem has been addressed by many able literary investigators, starting with William of Malmesbury, the most eminent early historian after the Venerable Bede, and his contemporary Geoffrey of Monmouth, a historical writer whose book *The History of the Kings of Britain* created more questions on history than it ever answered.

They were followed by the French romantic story tellers and fabulists of mediaeval times, including Sir Thomas Malory and his *Le Morte D'Arthur*, and others right through to the twentieth century, when there have appeared many books on the subject. Most writers agree that the characters, and in particular Arthur, were historic people.

All argue for different entities and locations, emphasising that there is no general agreement on who these historic ancestors were, nor indeed is there any great agreement on their particular time. Since they lived some 1,400 to 1,500 years ago, in a time known as the Dark Ages, this should not be surprising. Yet there are sufficient clues from these Dark Ages to enable an attempt to be made to thread the maze and come up with an answer of sorts, that seems to equate with what is accepted as known history.

This is one such attempt. It is not a history in the true sense, but is a historic scenario which suggests an explanation that could meet the

1

requirements of recognised or known events, in which Artur and his contemporaries fit, or sit in comfortably.

In our early history, the ancient Britons had little idea of kingship; they identified with the family type of relationship suggested by Chief or High Chief. Indeed, our word for king comes from the Saxon word *Cyng*, and was not adopted generally among the Britons until well into the seventh century. Hence the term 'King', as applied to Artur, is a misnomer and was a much later appendage.

The Teutonic tribes that Artur fought were a patrilineal society which had a sense of kingship, i.e., with some trappings of regality.

This was not so with the Britons. There is ample evidence that the Britons, in general, were a matrilineal society, where the Chieftaincy of the tribe was passed through the women of the clan, as evinced by Boudicca (Boadicea), Chieftainess of the Iceni, who took up this mantle after her husband Prasutagus died. She may, by her marriage, have bestowed the Chieftaincy on him.

Tacitus, the Roman historian, stated of Boudicca's famous rebellion, which was a great embarrassment to the patrilineal Romans, 'it was led by Boudicca, a woman of the Royal house [of the Iceni] – for the Britons do not distinguish between the sexes when it comes to military command.' Nor did they when clan chieftaincy was concerned: for example Cartimandua, Chieftainess of the Brigantes (the largest of all tribes in the land and a northern British tribe to boot), as well as others. They could either keep the Chieftaincy of the tribe to themselves or on marriage pass the responsibility for the leadership of the clan to their spouses.

Matrilineal societies are extremely old, and developed in times long, long ago, when it was not recognised the part men played in the procreation process; hence women, as the source of all life, were revered as the leaders of tribal societies, becoming 'Queens' and taking male consorts, who could be and often were sacrificed to tribal Gods.

This ancient custom, somewhat modified by later knowledge of male impregnation, was adhered to by the Celts right into historical times, and explains how sons of important British tribal families suddenly appear as chiefs and land owners in tribes many hundreds of miles from their home territory, by marrying with a female holding matrilineal succession rights to tribal lands and gaining, in some cases, the Chieftaincy without warfare or any form of subjection.

Many instances of this will be seen to occur, beginning with Aidan son of Gabhran of Scottish Dalriada, Artur's father, marrying into the British family of Clydno Eidyn, a Chief of the northern Britons, a 'Man of the North', of the *Gwyr* (Men) *Y* (of the) *Gogledd* (North), all names that will be met with and explained later. This was a good way of avoiding inbreeding in the principal families of the tribe.

The so-called Picts were the last tribes of the far northern Britons to continue this ancient tradition of matrilineal succession, albeit in an old and more individual way, by passing the leadership to the son of the present leader's sister.

The Roman historians tell us that the Caledonians of the north held both their wives and their children in common ownership among the tribe. This society gave much sexual freedom to both sexes, but in particular to the women, who, if the Chief became injured or infirm, would then bear children sired by younger and more vigorous candidates for the Chieftaincy.

This practice, because of the Roman occupation in the south, had been modified, and when the Romans left Britain, Chief females, as of old, again held the right to the title of clan or clan lands directly.

By the middle of the seventh century, the Britons were beginning to adopt the way of their Teutonic and Irish or Scottish neighbours, taking up a patrilineal way of son following father, and the title of King, instead of Chief, was just starting to be used.

There is a problem in deciding which is the right period to place Artur, he who united a number of British tribes to resist the invaders of these lands.

One of the earliest candidates who took on the Romans as invaders of the British Isles, in the first century, was Caractacus, Chief of the Catuvellauni and the Trinovantes tribes. He was nearly successful, worrying the Roman armies by brilliant guerrilla warfare over a period of nine years, but in the end Roman discipline won the day and Caractacus had to throw himself on the mercy of Cartimandua (Chieftainess of the Brigantes tribe), who had allied her tribe to the Roman way. He hoped she would intercede for him, but she immediately took him prisoner and handed him over to the Romans, such was her power.

Cartimandua divorced her husband, Venutius, in favour of his armour-bearer Vellocatus, and Venutius fermented a revolt against Cartimandua, but her friendship to the Romans paid off and they came to her aid, defeating Venutius and sustaining Cartimandua in her Chieftaincy.

She and Boudicca are the most famous of the British Chieftainesses. There are many others not so famous, such as Ethelfleda of Mercia, a British warrior 'Queen', and Gwenllian daughter of Gruffudd ap Cynan, who raised an army and fought the Anglo-Norman settlers in Wales, while in Ireland was 'Queen' Maeve (Medb) of Connaught, and perhaps even Gwenwhyvawr of the Cornovii of Rheged, Artur's wife (as suggested by Professor N.L. Goodrich in her book *King Arthur*), as well as those who left the leadership to their husbands.

The general consensus is that Artur's historical time stretched from the latter half of the fifth century to around the end of the sixth century, covering such personages as Ambrosius Aurelianus, victor at the battle of Mons Badonicus or Badonis (Mount or Hill of Badon or Bowden); Urien of Rheged, who united a number of British tribes to defeat the expansion of the Northumbrians; and recently, a minor chief of Powys, Owain Dangwyn (Eugein Dantguin) who is suggested as the historic Arthur in a book supporting a Welsh claim to him.

The crux of the argument, we feel, is settled by the 'Thirteen

Treasures of Britain', where five of the treasures are owned by our candidate's relatives in the north, and are mainly contemporary with his parents and grandparents.

The first treasure was owned by Ryderych Hael. It was a magical sword called Dyrnwyn which would burst into flames in the wrong hands. Note that no Arthurian magic sword called Excalibur or Caliburn is mentioned as a treasure of Britain. Ryderych is known to have lived in the sixth century, and was an adversary of Aidan, Artur's father.

Gwyddno Garanhir, son of Urien of Rheged, sixth century, of an age with Artur, had treasure number 2, a magical hamper. If food for one was put in, when reopened it would feed a multitude.

Clydno Eidyn, our Artur's grandfather, owned number 5, the treasure of a magic halter, which when fixed to the owner's bedstead, would in the morning have his favourite horse attached to it. He too lived in the sixth century. Note that there is no mention of Artur's wonderful horse as a treasure of Britain.

Ryderych Hael's father, Tutwal Tudclyd, also sixth century, possessed treasure number 8: a magic whetstone which, if a brave man sharpened his blade on it, would draw out the life of anyone wounded by it.

Lastly, Gwendalleau, chief of the Selgovae tribe, is quoted as possessing a magical chess board, treasure number 12, whose pieces played by themselves; he was killed at the battle of Arftyrydd fighting alongside Artur's father Aidan, c. AD 574.

If Artur had lived in the fifth century or earlier, then his magical accoutrements would surely have been included in the Treasures of Britain, e.g. his sword, horse and hounds. Their absence from Bardic verse, originating in the sixth century or later, must surely argue for Artur being of a later time, even though this may only be one or two generations after these 'Men of the North'.

Only treasure number 13 is given as Arthur's wonderful mantle or cloak. *This is an obvious insertion*, as the cloak that could bring invisibility was Caswallan's or Catwallan's, Chief of the Catuvellauni, first century, who fought the Roman general Platius in AD 43, and not Artur's.

Since the above named treasure owners are sixth century, surely this shows Artur to be of this particular time, the sixth century.

The remaining Treasures of Britain: number 3 was the horn of Bran which produced any drink one wanted. Number 4 was the chariot of Morgan the Wealthy, which would take you anywhere. Treasure number 6 was the knife of Llawfronedd the Horseman which could carve up two dozen men at a meal. Number 7 was the cauldron of Diwrnach the giant; it would not boil food for a coward. Treasure 9 was the coat of Padarn Red-Coat which would only fit a person of nobility. Numbers 10 and 11 were the crock and dish of Rhygenydd, where the food one liked best would always be found.

In an approach to the history of the ancient Britons of this time, one must forget Kings, Queens, Princes and Princesses, chivalrous knights, magic-making magicians, giants and magical beasts; these are the stuff of fairy tales, not plausible history, despite our use of the magical Treasures of Britain as a source of confirming a sixth century Artur and named persons relating to him.

There is enough early history of this period, contained in scraps of information, from which a credible explanation for the accepted, as known, facts can be deduced.

It is against this background that no apology is made for introducing yet another book on Artur (Arthur). Neither is it the first introduction of Artur, son of Aidan, son of Gabhran of Dalriada, on to this scene. He has generally been ignored as he was not a pure-bred Briton, without realising, it seems, that his grandmother was a Briton, his mother a Briton, that Artur himself married a woman of the Britons, so on his maternal side he is definitely of the Britons, sixth in descent from Coel Hen Godebog (Old King Cole) on the female side. (See Chapter 4.)

It all began in the mists of time, when a people who became known as Celts, that is to say, peoples who spoke a Celtic language, left the cradle of Indo-European civilisation, the Indus Valley, and moved northwards into Eastern Europe via Turkey, settling around the river Danube. Then began a great westward expansion through Germany and France, then known as Gaul.

These Gaulish Celts became known as 'P' Celtic or Britonic speaking, and were a trans-alpine people, whilst another branch who had made their way into Spain and Portugal, keeping south of the Alps, were known as 'Q' Celtic or Gaelic speaking.

The Gaulish Celts moved into the Channel Islands and from there, possibly via the Scilly Isles, to southern Ireland, as well as directly to Cornwall and Devon. They entered the Pritanic or Britanic Isles (Ynys Pryden) spreading north and eastwards, colonising the lands. The area of Gaul these migrants came from was known as Armorica, and there was for many years much to-ing and fro-ing between the south-west of England, south Wales, southern Ireland and even Albion or southern Scotland and continental Armorica.

In Ircland, the 'P' Brythonic speakers were known as the *Cruithne*, or Picts of Ireland.

This interaction was seriously curtailed by Roman imperialistic expansion into France, the Netherlands, and Saxony (Germany).

The Roman invasion of Spain and Portugal probably caused the pressures which brought the migration of the 'Q' Gaelic speaking Celts, the Scoti, into Ireland, over-running the earlier Cruithne and, much later, parts of the west coast of Britain.

This infusion of Britons on to the mainland, and Scoti in Ireland, into the indigenous populations, created pressures leading to the creation of groups, clans or tribes who were there when the Romans landed, the next great movement materially to affect the people of these Islands.

The Romans, having successfully invaded Britain, spread out north and west, though their principle route was north along the east coast, where their Legions could be supplied by sea, river and later, canal, overcoming the resistance of the Britons of the east.

Inroads into Scotland, then known as Albion or Pryden, in the earlier campaigns were temporarily successful, but with a substantial population of Britons in the south and Caledones in the northern regions, the military found it necessary to construct Hadrian's Wall. Later, the northern Antonine Wall was built which ran for thirty-seven miles between the River Clyde and the River Forth. With increasing raids from the north, the Antonine Wall was abandoned and then reoccupied on a number of occasions, but was eventually deserted.

When the Romans left Britain to its own devices in *c*. AD 410, a vacuum was created in the area roughly delineated by the two Roman Walls. A struggle for power ensued, wherein an Aidan, with his son Artur and others, became embroiled with those contending for power, i.e., Scots, Caledones or Picts, Northumbrians, Saxons and a series of British tribes, mainly Novantae, Cornovii, Selgovae, Damnonii, Maetae and the Gotadinii or Gododdin.

The resolution of all this turmoil was the final shape of modern England, Scotland, Wales and Ireland.

Out of all this, one Nennius, a Welsh monk or cleric, working near Bangor in north Wales at the beginning of the ninth century, resuscitated a poem or song by the early British bards, praising the exploits of a minor war leader called Arthur. This was taken up by Geoffrey of Monmouth in the twelfth century, who turned Arthur into a king, fabulised out of all proportion, in a book claiming to give the early history of the British nation. He was followed by others who made their tales into children's fairy stories, containing little of value in acceptable history, leading to the disarray, in general, of modern historical writers.

However, Nennius compiled a number of family genealogies of the Northern Britons, and a modern edition by P.C. Bartrum is titled *Early*

Welsh Genealogical Tracts. Here he expresses the opinion, with which we agree, that the early entries derived from the ancient bardic verbal sources are most likely to be authentic. Later entries by religious scribes who owed their livelihood to a petty Chief, and who in these later times, eighth century onwards, inserted various and spurious ancestors to please their mentors, are to be treated with great circumspection.

The ancient Welsh genealogies, based on Nennius's work in the early ninth century, do include a sixth century person, Arthur Benisal or Penisal, son of Eliffer Gosgordfawr, Chief of the Britons of Elmet, lands around York and Leeds, and his wife Elfryddl, daughter of Cynfarych O'Oer, head of the Chief family of the Selgovae tribe, in southern Scotland, lands around the Eildon Hills, and the forest and lands of Castle O'Oer.

Eliffer later had two other sons by another wife, Madrun (sister to Gwenwhyvawr, Gweniveve or Guinevere). Both these later sons became famous in British history; their exploits far outshone any accredited to their elder half-brother Arthur.

Eliffer, although not given as a 'Man of the North', is of a time with these heroes, and it is his son Gwrgi who is of the *Gwyr Y Gogledd*, and who is contemporary with Artur's generation.

One other named Arthur in the genealogies is Arthur son of Pedr, Petr or Reithoir, who was a grandson of Vortipor of Dyfed of the Dementae in the late sixth century and who is frequently mistaken for Artur of the North. Similarly, Vortipor of Dyfed is mistaken for Vortigern of the Cornovii based on Wroxeter. (See *The Figure of Arthur* by Dr Richard Barber.)

These are the odd occasions where a Welsh scribe has used an Artur spelling with an 'h'. The Welsh (Cambrian in the sixth century; they did not become known as Weala or Welsh till much later) spelling of Arthur would be Arddur ('dd' in Cambrian or Welsh is pronounced as 'th' in English).

Arthur son of Eliffer, and Arthur son of Pedr or Petr: the lack of exploits of these Arthurs must be the reason they are overlooked as candidates for the famous one. Not so with our candidate.

It may be interesting now to look at the laws of marriage and divorce of the Britons as set down in the tenth century by Hywell Dda, based on laws created originally by Dyfnwal Molemut, nephew of Dyfnwal Hen, a Chief of the northern Cymry in the sixth century and descended from Coel Hen Godebog.

This allowed a wife status after living with her partner for seven years; similarly, divorce was granted after seven years apart. Males could marry at fourteen years and females at twelve years, which explains much when working with the ancient genealogies. In truth they did not wait for these periods but divorced more often by mutual consent or even by force. Wives were accorded much status in Welsh law. If deserted by their husbands they could claim half of their property, whilst they could leave their husbands and still keep their dowry! Much sexual freedom was accepted as normal by both sexes.

Having mentioned the ancient Welsh genealogies, one must pay tribute to this amazing work, based on Nennius's original compilation, giving the family trees mainly of the *Northern Britons*. It includes many families whose lands were north of Hadrian's Wall, in southern Scotland, in northern England and North Wales, primarily of the Heroic Men of the North, the *Gwyr Y Gogledd*, the many descendants of Coel Hen Godebog. These people are to be met with later in our story.

It also included the genealogies of the Kings of Northumbria, i.e., those of Deira and Bernicia, which are now little used as it has been superseded by the *Anglo-Saxon Chronicle* and other dating information.

Nennius did include a few well known southern Welsh families, and, in particular, the Plant or children of Brychan of Brechiniog, now Brecon, probably the largest family in the whole tract. A number of

Brychan's children, particularly daughters, who seem to have been devout Christians, moved to southern Albion (Scotland), some founding religious establishments there, in a district known as Brechiniog of the north, modern Brechin in old Angus district or one time Forfarshire. This was probably due to the fame then of the Celtic Church as practised by St Ninnian of Candida Cassa, and his Christian missions to Cumbria and Wales (St Paldy, St David, St Illtud and St Samson being Candida Cassa trained, mostly by Paul Hen or St Paldoc: see A.B. Scott *The Pictish Nation, its People and Church*), as well as mainland Scotland, Northern Ireland (Bangor) and even into the Orkneys.

These genealogies included over two hundred entries of female lines, showing the importance of women in this matrilineal society.

The people the Romans found, therefore, when they invaded Britain, were pretty much, as far as the mainland was concerned, a homogeneous Brythonic speaking population, with the possible exception of the west coasts of Wales and Scotland. The majority of these people spoke 'P' Celtic, the language of the ancient Britons, somewhat as today with differing dialectic pronunciations. This made it difficult for the southern Saxon scribes, who wrote our early history, to recognise many place names, since their knowledge of British geography of places and names north of Hadrian's Wall was limited in the extreme, a syndrome still experienced today! If they found a British name that had a similarity to a known southern Saxon name, then that Saxon or English name was always adopted: e.g., Tinnis Castle, and Tantallon Castle in southern Scotland were ascribed to the Cornish Tintagel Castle. The present Tantallon Castle is of fourteenth century construction which has destroyed much evidence for an early Iron Age fort on the site, but the name 'Tantallon' is very ancient, derived probably from 'Temtalloun' or 'Thomptaloun'. It is protected on three sides by sheer cliffs down to the sea, leaving only one landward face to protect, an ideal Iron Age coastal fort situation. (Plate 1.)

His towers, Tantallon vast;
Broad, massive, high, and stretching far,
And held impregnable in war.
On a projecting rock they rose,
And round three sides the ocean flows,
The fourth did battle walls enclose,
And double mound and fosse.

Marmion, Canto fifth, by Sir Walter Scott.

Plate 1: Tantallon Castle

It is less well known that south-west Scotland has many place names beginning with Pol, Pen, Pin, Doon, and Calder or Cawder, like Cornwall, and they are a reminder of a branch of the Cornovii, who gave their name to Cornwall. Many of the happenings of this time, therefore, which were always ascribed to Cornwall, could equally well be set in the ancient districts of Dumfries and Galloway, the land of Rheged. Indeed, according to the Romans, there was a branch of the Cornovii in the most north-easterly corner of Scotland, in present-day Caithness – the Cornavii!

Modern researchers are somewhat careless about using general terms like 'Anglo Saxon' in a fifth or sixth century connotation. The Saxons of that time would have rough handled, or worse, Teutons of the other settling tribes whom they called Angles, be they Jute, Frisian, or Ingle (who became the Northumbrians, the Logres of Logria or English) should they take umbrage at them.

These tribes did not unite properly until shortly after the death of King Alfred, who had united the various Saxon tribes. Then, to meet the threat of Viking invasion at the beginning of the ninth century, the Saxons joined with the Northumbrians and then formed the Anglo-Saxon nation, which lasted some one and a half centuries before the Norman invasion of AD 1066, which Normanised the Anglo-Saxons, eventually to become the English.

T.W. Rolleston in his book *Celtic Myths and Legends*, suggests that the term Anglo Celtic, rather than Anglo Saxon, would be a much better description for the English nation! Both Angles and Saxons were descended from a common Teutonic ancestral tribe, and were similar to each other as indeed were the other Teutonic tribes, the Jutes and Frisians, who all inter-married with the early Brythons.

An even worse general term is that of Pict, or Picti, now known as the painted people. It certainly was not a term used generally during the Roman occupation, when Roman geographers carried out a number of surveys of the whole land. Those people north of the Antonine Wall were given the general term Caledones, a name always preferred by the most knowledgeable of the Roman and Greek historians, Tacitus, Ptolemy, Dio Cassius, and Herodian. None of these eminent historians ever used the term Picts, but always Caledones or Dicaledones.

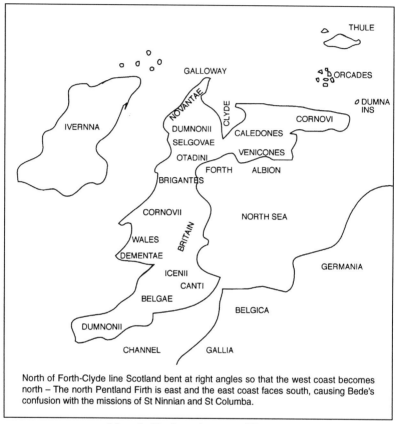

Map 1: Ptolemy's map of Britain

It first appears as a name in *c.* AD 279, where one Eumenius describes the Picti and the Hibernii as enemies of the Britons. The term Pict or Picti, it is suggested, was first used by Roman soldiers on the Walls as a nickname, but it is most unlikely that a nickname would give rise to the naming of a whole people.

Boudicca of the Iceni painted herself with woad yet she is never referred to as a Pict, and well south of any of the Walls, in Powys, was a Chief called Tidlet of the *Picts of Powys*! They were not therefore restricted to north of the Antonine Wall. In fact Prawst, the daughter of Tidlet or Tithlym, Chief of the Powy's Picts, married Enion Yrth, son of Cunedda Weldig and so was Owain Dangwyn's mother, making him half Pictish! (A Welsh candidate for a historic Arthur, see Chapter 14).

The Brythonic term *Brythwyr*, meaning 'speckled ones', is a more understandable term, which could apply to Gaels with red hair who have a genetic propensity to freckles (the Gwydell Fichti, for example, a mixed race of Irish and Briton); more likely, it is the use of tattooing using dots or speckles to make up the design which gave rise to this name. The term for 'painted' is *Agned*, as in *Mont Agned*, 'the painted mount', now Artur's Seat in Edinburgh.

It would appear that the name used by these people was Pecht, or Pechti, as in Pechtland (now Pentland) Firth, and Pechtland (now Pentland) Hills. However, there were two types of Pecht, the most numerous speaking a dialect of 'P' Celtic, somewhat akin to Gaulish, which would suggest that they were an earlier wave of the people from Gaul (Armorica). The number of Brythonic names still to be found in the lands of the Northern Picts, particularly the term Aber as in Aberdeen and a multiplicity of other Abers, a purely British or Welsh word, gives credence to their Brythonic origins.

As for the other and smaller, territorially speaking, people, it is not quite clear what their language was. In this hypothesis it is suggested it might have been Gaelic or 'Q' Celtic. The over-running of Pictland by the 'Q' speaking Dalriadic Scots in the ninth century, led by Kenneth MacAlpine, has tended to blot out the earlier evidence for 'Q' speaking Pechts.

During the sixth century they were known as the Gwyddel Ffichti in Wales and along the line of the Antonine Wall, speaking a strange dialect, a mixture of British (Cumbric or Welsh) and Irish.

The river and town of Annan, on the north side of the Solway Firth, was named after the ancient Celtic God Annun or Annwn, God of the underworld, with the loch, town and stone of Mabon (Mabenstane) nearby, named after another early Celtic God (Artur rescues the God King Mabon in the tale of 'Culhwch and Olwen'). In the same vicinity lies the Dun of Rheged (Dun Raggit), another very ancient British demi-god. Lastly, just north in Ayrshire is Lugton, the God Llud (Lleu) or Llug's town. All these examples suggest that this earlier wave of 'P' speaking Celtic peoples had been driven to the north by the later waves of the Britons and later 'P' speakers, leaving these early and very ancient names in what is now southern Scotland.

In the book of Taliesin is the story of Artur raiding the 'Spoils of Annwn' which was called the fort of Glass, Caer Wydyr, another name for the underworld. It was supposedly in Ireland, but the Cruithne of Ireland occupied much of the Rhins of Galloway and it might in those times have been considered as part of Ireland, with the mists and dangerous waters and quicksands of the Solway Firth seen from the Cumbrian coast as the underworld (Annwn) or land of Gorre.

Next to present day Annan is Glasserton, Glass or Glasser's town or fort.

The *Pictish Chronicle*, which survived via the *Iona Chronicle* which had been taken to Bangor, Northern Ireland, lists the Kings of the Picts, going back to the time before the Romans arrived. On their arrival, their King Brude Grid (Cridus) attacked Caesar in 54 BC, hence these Picts must have inhabited the south coast of England. Later Gilgig or Galgac(us) fought Agricola in his Scottish campaigns in AD 83, as reported on by Tacitus who states that Galgacus called his people Britanni or Pritanni, showing that the Picts were of the race of the Britons.

Their term *Brude* meant 'speaker', and later became the name for 'leader'. In the very far north it was often pronounced as Bredi.

Indeed the last vestiges of the British way of matrilineal succession was adhered to by the ancient Caledones or the people now termed Picts, right up to the ninth century when they came under the influence of the Scots of Dalriada, forming the embryonic Kingdom of Scotland.

Kenneth MacAlpine, King in Dalriada, who united the Picts and the Scots in the ninth century, was only able to do this as his grandfather had married a Pictish noble woman, and because of this relationship, he claimed the Chieftaincy of the Picts through her.

Artur's younger brother Gartnait (see Table 2 for Arthur's family tree), married a Pictish Chieftainess and was the start of the Scots claims via matrilineal succession to the leadership of the northern Caledone or Pictish peoples. In many of the lines of the Dalriadic Scots appear Pictish names, as evinced by Gartnait himself, a typical Pictish name, showing a fair degree of intermarriage between Iro-Scot and Brito-Pict or Caledonian.

The stage has now been set for the story of Artur the Warrior, son of Aidan Mac Gabhran, a sixth century person, a real historic person of this actual name.

CHAPTER 1

THE LEGENDS OF ARTHUR

On either side the river lie
Long fields of barley and of rye,
That clothe the wold and meet the sky;
and thro' the field the road runs bye
To many-tower'd Camelot;

Tennyson: 'The Lady of Shalott'

We begin by looking at the state of the Arthurian legends as they stand today in the latter half of the twentieth century, based initially on a few verses by the ancient Brythonic bards about an early war leader called Arthur who fought the Saesons or Saxsons, a generalistic name used by the Britons for the Teutonic tribes that invaded the Isles of Britain.

This work was rediscovered by a Welsh Cleric, now called Nennius, at the beginning of the ninth century, when the land was once again under threat of Viking invasion and in need of a heroic figure to sustain the inhabitants in their stand against these pagan Norsemen.

This started a grass roots folklore on the person of Arthur, culminating in the twelfth century, when one Geoffrey of Monmouth, in his book *The History of the Kings of Britain*, made Arthur a King of Britain, son of an Uther Pendragon, a King or Chieftain, living in the latter half of the fifth to around the early part of the sixth century, and residing anywhere from Devon or Cornwall, through Wales or, in the North, in old Westmorland now Cumbria, to even possibly southern Scotland; almost the whole span of anywhere in the country.

From this basis sprang three mainstream groups of legends. The first were the French romantic writers who got their Arthur stories from the Breton settlers of 'Little Britain', now Brittany, where Arthur resided in a forest of Broceliande, a geographical location that the French have never proved to exist. There is a good case for this forest being in Scotland, part of the old Caledonian wood, in the realm of King Ban of Benioc, father of Sir Lancelot du Lac of Écosse (Scotland). Mallory makes him King Ban of Benwick (probably Berwick).

They introduced the concept of mediaeval chivalry, of jousting and knightly valour, rescuing maidens in distress. Despite this, these writers gave Arthur's wife Guinivere (Gwenwhyvawr) a very bad press, making her out to be of a very promiscuous nature.

Wace, a native of Jersey, introduced the idea of the Round Table, while Chrétien de Troyes in his *Conte del Graal* or *Perceval de Gallois* brought in the search for the Holy Grail, supposedly carried to Britain or Brittany by Joseph of Arimathea, and much expanded by Robert de Baron who first describes it as a Christian object.

In the Welsh tales, the magic cauldron in which soldiers killed could be revived by insertion into its maw resided in Ireland or Annwn the underworld. It equates with the Holy Grail of the Breton stories.

Arthur dispatched his best Knights in the search for the Holy Grail, Sir Galahad and Sir Percival (Peredur in Brythonic). Percival finally achieves entry to the Grail castle, and finds the Grail itself, by asking the right question.

The second category comprises the Welsh Mabinogion stories, where Arthur is mixed up very much with the mythical characters of the creation myths and gods of the Celtic tribes. In these stories Arthur is not always a 'nice' personality, but in many cases quite the reverse.

The French romance stories, introduced into Wales in the twelfth century, did not in general agree with the early Welsh tales, and were therefore much ignored, although these stories were derived from tales that had been taken to Brittany in the sixth and later centuries when there was much interchange of culture between the Celtic west of Britain and Brittany.

The last group is epitomised by Sir Thomas Mallory in his work *Le Morte D'Arthur*, from which are derived the most popularly known tales, as far as the English speaking world is concerned. Arthur comes across the sword in the stone in London. He alone is able to withdraw the weapon and so becomes, as foretold, the true King of England, this despite the fact that most acceptable histories show Arthur to be involved in fighting the Saxon and other Teutonic invaders that occupied much of eastern Britain.

Arthur, now generally accepted as a 'King' and, in general, of some apparent virtue, unfortunately, in devious circumstances created by the witch Morganna or Morgan Le Fay, sister to Loth of Lothian, had sexual relations with his own sister Gwyar, wife of Loth. In due course she produced a son, Modred or Medraut. Other versions have Morgan Le Fay as Arthur's sister, and wife to Loth, who by her magic induces Arthur to lie with her, conceiving Modred.

Loth does not appear to be aware of the circumstances of this event, whilst Modred, as he grows up, leaves Lothian to join Arthur's court at Camelot (Camelon), and seems to be aware of his paternity, constantly plotting against his uncle or incestuous parent.

Gwenwhyvawr (Brythonic), Gwenieve (English) or Guinevere (French), Arthur's wife, is of a flirtatious disposition, but eventually falls under the spell of Sir Lancelot Du Lac, and they become lovers. Modred manages to appraise Arthur of the situation, causing enmity between him and Sir Lancelot, his most favoured knight.

Arthur then brings Sir Lancelot, in alliance with Modred, to battle, and defeats them, although he is mortally wounded in the fight and commands Sir Bedevere to dispose of his famous sword Caliburn or Excalibur, by throwing it into the nearby lake.

Bedevere has to be commanded three times before he concedes to Arthur's last order and finally throws wondrous Excalibur into the lake. A hand is seen to come out of the water to seize the sword and take it into the care of the water deities; whereupon out of the mists comes a boat rowed by the maidens of the Lake, who take Arthur to an under- or other-worldly place, the island of Avalon, to heal his wounds and keep him in perpetuity or until Britain is once again invaded and in need of his heroic services.

Some versions have Arthur and his men asleep deep in a cavern or hillside to be awakened by a clarion call, to return once again to save Britain from some peril. One such version has Artur under the Eildon hills in southern Scotland.

Throughout all this flits the elusive character of the magician Merlin, or British Myrddin (for whom there is as much historical evidence as there is for an Arthur), famed for his shape-changing abilities, who by his magic had helped Arthur's father Uther Pendragon to lie with Ygerne wife of Gorlois, a Chief in Cornwall, so fathering Arthur, by making Uther in the likeness of her husband; in return Merlin made Uther swear on the names of the four evangelists to give up the son that would be born of this union to him, for his upbringing.

However, on the night that they lay together and conceived Arthur, Gorlois had been killed on the field of battle, that very day and so, when told of her husband's death, Ygerne realised that the person in her husband's likeness whom she had slept with could not have been her true spouse. Yet because of Uther's love for her, she married him.

Merlin defeats the machinations of Morganna against Arthur in a great battle of shape changing, cleverly portrayed in the Disney cartoon *The Sword in the Stone*.

Apart from these three main Arthurian sources, there were many coincidental tales that impinged on Arthur, the most famous being the tale of Tristan and Iseult, a Pictish or northern tale, adopted as a Cornish story because there was a stone (Cunomorus Stone) with a Tristan inscription on it in Cornwall, stating 'Here lies Drustanus son of Cunomorus'. Drustanus is equated with Tristan, but is in fact the popular Pictish name Drurst latinised into Drustanus, and there were more than eight kings of this name among the northern Picts. Cunomorus is a Brito-Pictish name from Mannau Gododdin, from which is derived the Brythonic name Cynvelyn or Cunobelinus; one of this name was a man of Dun Eidin, Edinburgh.

It is possible that the tale of Sir Gawain and the Green Knight was a very early story, pre-dating Geoffrey of Monmouth's work. In it a Knight in green comes to Arthur's hall seeking anyone to trade blows with him. Sir Gawain, or Gwalchmai son of Loth, Arthur's nephew, accepts the dare and, striking the first blow, cuts off the Knight's head, whereupon the Knight picks up his head and requests that Gawain meet him on New Year's Day, to receive his return blow.

On his way to this assignment Gawain stays with a nobleman and each agrees to give to the other whatever they received each day. On the first day Gawain is given a kiss from the wife to pass on to her husband, who has gone on a hunt, which Gawain duly does; on the second day he receives two kisses to pass on, and again he does so; whilst on the third day, he receives three kisses from his host's wife plus some green material which by magic will prevent him being killed or seriously wounded; the three kisses he passes on but keeps the material to himself.

Continuing on his way to the chapel of the Green Knight, the place of their meeting, he arrives, where he presents his head for the Green Knight's blow, but is secretly protected by the magic cloth. The Knight strikes twice, missing Gawain, but his third blow only slightly cuts his neck. The Green Knight reveals his identity as his host of the previous evenings, and declares he would not have struck

Gawain if he had given up, as promised, everything that had been given him.

Over the years numerous poems have been written describing Arthur and his many Knights and their adventures, from Spenser's *Faerie Queene* to Tennyson's *Idylls of the King*, with an explosion of such works in the nineteenth century. Even Shakespere got in on the Arthurian scene, with his *King Lear*, i.e. Llew or Loth of Lothian.

These then are the basic stories that have to be searched for the historical veracity of an Arthur and his contemporaries.

Chapter 2

The Trouble with Legends...

My good blade carves the casques of men,
My tough lance thrusteth sure,
My strength is of the strength of ten,
Because my heart is pure.

Tennyson: 'Sir Galahad'

Having restated the basic stories it will be necessary to examine them
to see if they have any basis in a historical context.

The biggest drawback to this is that the stories are obvious fairy
tales, crammed with full-blown witches and wizards and lesser
practitioners of the other-worldly arts, learned in the first instance
from ancient gods.

They contain magical beasts such as the great Boar of Britain, Twrch
Trwyth, whom Arthur with his retainers chases throughout the whole
length and breadth of the land, until it reaches the south coast, where
it plunges into the Channel and swims to Brittany in France, still
chased by Arthur.

There are giants like Yspadden, who prevents his beautiful daughter
Olwen from marrying anyone, as on her marriage he will die; so suitors
are always set impossible tasks. Culhwch, however, in the tale of
'Culhwch and Olwen' eventually carries out these deeds with the help
of a little magic, so securing Olwen's hand.

Despite this, description of the places harbouring much of the action allows recognition of some real localities, and helps to start off a historical search for the real people behind the fables.

We will look first at the time period, with the chivalrous notions of the Knights of the Round Table, their courtly manners and their pure and chaste love, although they are constantly forced into sleeping with damsels they do not want, through, of course, from no fault of their own. An example is Sir Launcelot fathering Sir Galahad on Dame Elaine. This immediately suggests the mediaeval historical period, but as the time of their writing down includes the twelfth to the fifteenth centuries and describes people of a much earlier age, the authors have fallen into a trap of their own making in believing, naively, that their own time has always been the way of earlier ages, because their knowledge of antiquity was very limited.

We know of course, that this is not the case.

Each of the tripartite source legends naturally locates Arthur in its own locality: the Mabinogion tales in Cambria, which encompassed Wales, Cornwall, Devon in the south and Cumbria in the north which included southern Scotland with Northumberland; the French, naturally, in Brittany; and Mallory in the east in Saxon England. In Arthur's time, however, fifth to sixth centuries, there was no such place known as England then in existence; similarly with Wales and Scotland.

This geographical spread obviously invites investigation into whether Arthur could possibly have roamed in all three locations.

At this time, the end of the fifth and into the sixth century, there was certainly much interchange of peoples and cultures from south-west England, Wales and Ireland, and indeed Scotland, which country has from such times kept a close relationship with France, the Auld Alliance of its battles against the English.

Probably the son of Caw of Pryden, Gildas Albanus sojourned to Armorica (an early name for Gaul) at this time, as did St Samson, another of Caw's sons. It is therefore quite possible for Arthur to have travelled to Brittany or southern England; however, it is much more likely that stories of an Arthur and his prowess were carried there by word of mouth, with the interchange of peoples, due in no small degree to Saxon aggression pressing at this time ever westwards, causing a refugee traffic to the continent, particularly in the south. This scene argues against the French and Saxon claims to be the land of the original Arthur.

In all three types of legend, the Knights are continually not recognising their fellow Knights and so getting into fights with each other, in some cases considerably wounding or killing their friends, even though each supposedly carries his coat of arms on his shield, on his flag or on the pennant flown either by himself or his squire. This means they were deliberately blind to each other's identity, and human jealousy or other dislikes were the real causes of this internecine warfare. The killing of Sir Balan by his brother Sir Balin, the slaying of Sir Elias by Sir Tristram and the fight between Sir Gareth and Sir Gawain are examples.

Again it could be said that in many of the stories Arthur did not lead from the front, and that the tempo of chivalry of the Round Table as accepted today was, if the fables are examined closely, a veritable myth. This was certainly true in the case of many of the Welsh Mabinogion tales.

On a number of occasions, Arthur leads his men into battle with disastrous results, such as his expedition to the Spoils of Annwn where three boat-loads depart but only seven warriors return, and in his last battle where he manages to get himself mortally wounded, despite the protection of his wondrous sword Caliburn or Excalibur, and where apparently only he and Sir Bedivere are left on the field of the fray. These stories do not lead us to believe him to be a very good tactical leader in battle, but this was probably due to Merlin (Myrddin) deserting him on occasions, leaving him to his own devices. It does not equate very well with Nennius's victorious leader of twelve battles, who in one instance killed some nine hundred or more of his enemies, bringing peace to his land. This work of Nennius gives a historical basis to the stories of an Arthur.

When Merlin offers to help Uther Pendragon, a King of England according to Mallory, lie with Ygerne, he makes Uther swear on the names of the four evangelists, though Merlin or Myrddin, a Chief Druid, would know little about Christian evangelists. This shows how much the ancient stories had been taken over by later mediaeval Christian society, thus affecting how the mediaeval writers and poets portrayed their characters with a definite religious bias that was not recognisable in the earlier Christian days of the original stories.

The Romans did not mention any Hero King of this actual name, either in Britain or in continental Europe, so it can be assumed that Artur's period was after the departure of the Romans from Britain in the early part of the fifth century, as far as a British Arthur is concerned, and some considerable time later, when the Romans withdrew from continental Gaul, for an Armorican or Gaulish Arthur, so dating him to some time between the fifth and the seventh century.

Alternatively it could be assumed that Arthur was not his real name but an endearing nickname, as suggested by Professor N.L. Goodrich, who proclaims 'Artir' means 'Father', and so he was father to his people, for bringing peace and prosperity out of chaos.

This then opens the field up to a wide range of possible candidates, from Caractacus in the first century fighting the Roman invaders to Urien of Rheged engaging and defeating the Angles of Northumbria in the sixth century, and perhaps Cadwallon in the seventh century, who also fought the Northumbrians.

However, in these fables there can be recognised a number of Brythonic names associated with Arthur that can be attributed to Dark Age Britain, so well before the time of mediaeval Kings, Queens, Knights and chaste or courtly ladies, confirming the antiquity of the source material for the romance stories. It is from these ancient names, handed down by bardic recitation, that we can begin to establish the veracity of a historical Arthur and others of his time.

As good a place to start as any, is to look at the name 'Artur'. It is often accepted today that it is derived from the Roman or Latin name Artorius or Arturus. The suffix in Latin '*us*' denotes a male gender name, thus leaving Artori or Artur as his basic name. In fact, names beginning with 'Art' are quite common among the European Celtic tribes, for example Gaul, Artaius, God of the Gauls, as well as in Britain, Artur, Arthur or Arddur; and even among the Irish, the third century High King, Cormac Mac Art, son of Art son of Con, who drove the Dessi tribe out of Ireland, forcing them to settle among the Dementae of Dyfed in south Wales, under the leadership of Eochaid, son of Artchorp. Descended from him is Arthur son of Retheoir, Pedr or Petr, i.e. Arthur of Dyfed. (See *The Figure of Arthur* by Dr Richard Barber.)

From this it can be seen that there is a wide range of 'Art-' names, suggesting that the greatest likelihood is for a derivation of 'Art' being his real name, like Artur son of Aidan Mac Gabhran.

This settlement of the Irish into the west coast of Wales introduced Irish myth into the folklore of the Welsh, and there are many parallels to these Irish myths in the Mabinogion stories.

The early Irish have a lot of 'Art' names and, significantly, both Artur of Dyfed and Artur of Dalriada are descended from Irish Clans.

The insertion of an 'h' into the name would appear to be of Saxon origin; it did not occur in any of the Latin or Celtic forms.

CHAPTER 3

LINKING THE LEGENDS
TO THE HISTORIC

...when usurers till their gold i' the field;
And bawds and whores do churches build;-
Then shall the realm of Albion
come to great confusion.

Shakespere

We have suggested in the last chapter two possible avenues down which investigations for the historical authenticity of Arthur and close associates can be followed: namely, locations or place names and the ancient Brythonic personal names to be found in the early Welsh genealogical tracts, particularly those names before the eighth century, relying solely on the bards of the Britons and their method of training to recite by rote, with a high degree of accuracy, many family genealogies.

In dealing with place names, one must remember that much of Brythonic England and Scotland was over-run by the Teutonic tribes of the Angles, Saxons, Frisians and Jutes, whose language, Anglo Saxon, replaced much of the ancient Cambrian (old Welsh, or more correctly old British) or Cumbric, its equivalent dialect in the north, leaving today only Welsh, the modern version of the old British tongue. This does cause some confusion, when places suggest locations in the south whilst genealogical names suggest districts in the north, and vice versa. An example of this is that in the south the term for 'fort' is always *Caer* as in Caerphilly, but in the north it is sometimes *Car* as in Carlisle (Caer Llion, a fort of the legions, ruled by Lady Lionesse) and Carstairs, a Roman fort.

Even more confusion reigns when a number of place names have a variety of geographical sites with the same or similar name: Badon, Bawdon or Bowdon, as a good example, all pronounced as *B-awe-don.*

Which locale does one choose as the correct location?

A further help to the researcher is that the Romans named the tribes they found inhabiting Britain, and even delineated their tribal boundaries (see Map 2: Scottish tribes), sometimes putting speeches into the mouths of their leaders, another source of early personal names.

There were also, of course, the early historians, from the Greeks and the Romans to the Briton St Gildas and the Iro-Scot St Adamnan, these latter two living in the sixth and seventh centuries.

St Gildas, contemporary with the time of Arthur, does not mention any famous person of this name, but does mention a great British battle, defeating the invading Saxons, who assisted a British Tyranus (later identified by Nennius as Vortigern, Chief of the Cornovii tribe), at a Mount or Hill of Badon, which he latinised into the battle of Mons Badonicus. Here the Britons, led by their leader Ambrosius Aurelianus, had a great victory so that the Saxons and others, for a considerable time afterwards, left the Britons in peace. This fact was rediscovered by Nennius at the beginning of the ninth century, so starting a folklore that culminated in the romantic Arthurian stories of mediaeval times.

St Adamnan, writing in the seventh century, almost within living memory of Arthur's time, actually names a historic person, Artur son of Aidan of the Dalriadic Scots, in the time of St Columba, the most powerful prelate of the sixth century and a contemporary of Artur and St Gildas. It is here that we learn much of the swashbuckling Aidan, King of Dalriada, whose children, including one named Artur, were set an example by their father and other Heroic Men of the North, the Gwyr Y Gogledd, earning them, and especially Artur, a Hero's epic poem by the Brythonic Bards.

Some of the best sources are early Irish folk tales and historical annals, written down by their monks and taken in many cases to Armorica, which stories were unadulterated by foreign intrusions until the late eighth and early ninth century when Ireland was attacked by Viking raiders. The settlement by the Irish into south-west England, west Wales and other western parts of the mainland in the fourth century brought about an intermixing of the early mythic fables of both nationalities.

In many of the tales are decidedly northern personalities, such as Bellicent, Queen of Orkney and Lothian, first wife of Loth, and their sons Beaumains (otherwise Sir Gareth) and Modred, whilst Sir Gawain or Gwalchmai was son of Loth by his second marriage to Arthur's sister Gwyar, all very Brythonic names. They fought a 'King' Clariance of Northumberland, and a 'King' Urience (Urien), who was Sir Uwain's (Owain) father, King of Rheged or Gorre, to name just two.

Localities can be recognised, for example when Sir Launcelot brought Sir Tristram and La Beal Isoud into England, i.e., Northumberland and took them to Joyous Garde or Dinguroy (Bambro' Castle). Another case was when Sir Dinadan and others came to Humber Bank, and took ship, all describing northern places.

One point with which great care must be taken is the frequent statement 'they came over the sea', or 'went over the sea'. This should not be taken literally, as in those times travel by land was very difficult and passage by sea and river was a much easier choice. The Picts when raiding to the south came over the sea. It does not necessarily mean over the sea from a different country, and this can put a different complexion on many an interpretation for a locality.

From this background, we argue a case for this Artur of the North, son of Aidan, son of Gabhran, as the true historic model of the later Arthurian tales; taking the scope further, to include the authenticity of his wife Gwenwhyvawr, daughter of Gwrtheyrn Gwrtheneu, advisor to Urien of Rheged and Myrddin (Merlin), son of Morken of Alcluyd, sage of the northern Selgovae tribe and comrade in arms to Artur's father at the great battle of Arftyrydd, all in the sixth century.

We start our investigations with one of Artur's earliest ancestors, Coel Hen Godebog, Old King Cole of nursery rhyme fame, and from there move to the earliest historians St Gildas and St Adamnan, through the life of his father Aidan, to Artur himself; then to Myrddin, with a small chapter squeezed in between on Nennius, who rediscovered Artur in the early ninth century. After this we discuss other historians down to the present time, concluding with a restatement of the main points of our argument.

CHAPTER 4

COEL HEN GODEBOG

Our auld King Coul was a jolly auld saul
and a jolly auld saul was he
our auld King Coul fill'd a jolly brown bowl
and he ca'd for his fiddlers three
fidell didell, fidell didell quo' the fiddlers
there's no a lass in a' Scotland
like our sweet Marjorie.

Anon

In starting our search for the historic person of an Artur, as against the Arthur of the fabulised and magical tales of the mediaeval story-tellers, we begin with the state of northern Britain (north of the Hadrian Wall) when the Romans left around AD 410. They had left in the north a powerful Over or High Chief called Coel Hen Godebog or Gautopec, who took on the mantle of a Roman Dux Britannarium. He was a northern Dux, remembered to this day in the nursery rhymes about an Old King Cole. (Artur is sixth in descent from him on his mother's side.)

The above version of the 'Old King Cole' nursery rhyme is the oldest version known, written in Doric or Lallan Scots. It certainly would appear that the poem is describing a King who at one time lived in Scotland. This version was the favourite of Robert Burns who collected many of the ancient rhymes.

Coel's name is a good example of the variations in spelling which caused much confusion in later times, at least six names being applicable to the same person. Worse, Coel was also a popular name among the Britons, and so difficult to isolate:

Saxon:	Cole.
Latinised Saxon:	Coleius.
Britonic:	Coil.
Latinised Britonic:	Coilius.
Dilectic Britonic:	Coel (most used spelling).
Northern Britonic:	Coyl, or Cyl or Kyl; these latter two spellings are pronounced as Kyle.

Kyle is the district in Ayrshire remembering this ancient Chief to this day, the Chief who instead of a nursery rhyme deserves his title of King.

The Romans in their invasion of the British Isles eventually penetrated into the lands of the north, known today as Scotland, around AD 80. There they found that it was difficult to sustain a large army in such rough terrain, and fell back to the line from the River Tyne in the east to the Solway Firth in the west, where in *c.* AD 120 Hadrian constructed his famous wall.

This did not mean that they had abandoned the occupation of the lands to the north of the wall. Indeed, some twenty-odd years later, in *c.* AD 143, they constructed the Antonine Wall, on a line from the River Clyde to the Forth. This defence was of a much lighter construction than the Hadrian Wall but was found to be satisfactory, as the Caledones or Picts north of the wall, when raiding to the south, did their raiding by sea, thus circumventing both this fortification and Hadrian's Wall. This showed they were indeed substantial land barriers.

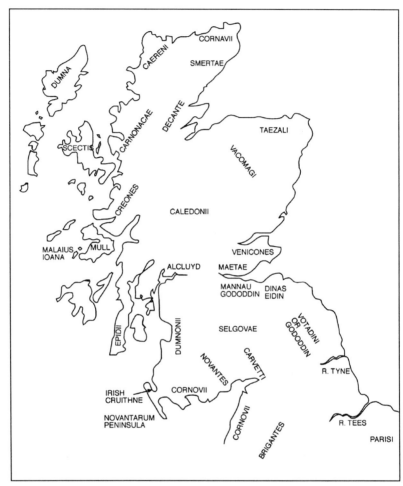

Map 2: The Tribes of Scotland named by the Romans

What caused the Romans to abandon Antonine's Wall was the difficulty of keeping it supplied. Eventually, there was also the need for more troops in the south to deal with uprisings and finally the threat of Saxon invasion. This meant that they had only a limited control over the British tribes situated between these two walls.

In these circumstances, where the Roman sway with the local tribes was tenuous to say the least, they supported a High or Over Chief to unite the tribes and keep them friendly to the Roman presence. Thus they act as a buffer state against, in this case, the northern Caledones or Picts, and the Scoti from Ireland. In return for this, they received Roman gold, Roman trade and the promise of Roman military protection. These High Chiefs were given the Roman title of Praefectus.

Such a Praefectus was Coel Hen Godebog (the wise, the protector), from the tribal lands of Aeron or Arwyr (Ayrshire). He wielded an amalgam of tribes between the two walls and beyond into a powerful British protectorate, stretching possibly from Loch Lomond (Loch Llumonyw) to York, a considerable territory. This confederacy of tribes, Coel held together after the Romans left in AD 410. Coel was acting as a true northern Dux, termed in the Britonic language Weldig (War Chief) or Saxonised into Gueldig.

However, this buffer zone was attacked in the west by the Iro-Scots, and in the north-east by the Caledones or Picts, so that Coel had his hands full, but survived well. He was eventually killed in battle around AD 430, some twenty years after the Romans had left, by the Irish King Nath I mac Fiachrach at the battle of Coilsfield in present day Ayrshire. Nath was probably supporting a small group of Iro-Scots who had tried to colonise around the mouth of the River Doon in Ayrshire. Although Coel Hen was defeated, it is not known whether the colony survived or not.

After Coel's death around AD 430, in time his conglomerate of tribes began to break up into smaller tribal lands, usually having as their Chiefs descendants of Coel Hen.

The largest of these clan lands was Rheged, under the chieftaincy in the sixth century of Urien. This tribal land was inhabited by the peoples of the Novantae, named after the Novantarum Peninsula, or the New Peninsula. This was the Mull of Galloway, named by the Romans after their fleet did a circumnavigation of the British Isles in the first century, populated by the Cornovii, the Carvetii, some Selgovae, some

37

Brigantes, and perhaps others. This territory was not formed by force of arms and so, perhaps, was the last and biggest remnant of Coel's influence.

More interesting, well to the north of Urien's Rhegd, separated by smaller tribal groups and ruled over by Coel's descendants, was a territory known as Northern Rheged. It lay around Loch Lomond and Lennox (Loch Llumonyw and Linneas), which suggests that at one time Rheged covered the whole south-west of Scotland, under Coel's power, and at its peak stretched from Loch Lomond to York.

These tribes in general were nominally Christian, after the administrations of St Ninnian of Candida Cassa, whose mission was set up in AD 397. He had sent out his missionaries to spread Christianity throughout the land, right up into the Island of Orkney, to Bangor in Northern Ireland, and to Cumbria and Wales, at the end of the fourth and into the fifth and sixth centuries. It would appear that this new religion existed peacefully with the old Druidic one in many places.

These Praefecti or Weldigs often founded their own dynastic lines. That of Coel, some five or six generations after him, became famous as the 'Thirteen Heroic Men of the North', the *Gwyr Y Gogledd* (five generations), and their illustrious sons (six generations). They by their exploits, not against the Saxons in general but mainly against the Inglis or Northumbrians, Iro-Scots and Caledons or Picts, gave new hope to the ancient tribes of the Britons, the Combrogi (fellow countrymen) or Cymry, that the Teutonic and other invaders could, and would, be driven from their land.

This brought a resurgence of bardic song and epic poetry, repeated in the halls of their descendants to inspire them to similar feats of heroism. Indeed, in the seventh century, the Welsh Chief Cadwallon of Gwynedd made a mighty effort against the Northumbrians, when he had a pact with Penda of Mercia, and defeated Edwin of Northumbria at Hatfield Chase in *c.* 632, in the old heroic mould. His was the last great Britonic effort against the Angles or Inglis of the north. Unfortunately Oswald, Edwin's successor, caught Cadwallon by chance near Hexham and killed him.

After this it was up to the Scots who by a hair's breadth, some centuries later, kept their independence.

It is a great pity that little is taught in Scottish schools about these early British ancestors, who became the Heroic Men of the North, the *Gwyr Y Gogledd*. They are still remembered to this day in many place names in southern Scotland, Albion or Pryden.

The exploits of these descendants or 'Whelps of Coel' were being sung about in the halls of the Welsh clans when Gildas was writing his history of complaints against the British Chiefs (see Chapter 5). But he did not listen to such irrelevances and missed the exploits of one called Artur, and the populace had to await Nennius's revelations on a war leader called Artur, some three centuries later.

It is to the Welsh or British bards that one has to turn to for confirmation of this once famous leader. In the poem 'The Gododdin' by Aneirin, the British leaders are referred to as 'The sons of Coel'. In another poem recounting a battle probably in Cumbria or on the north-eastern shore of Loch Lomond (Argoed Llwyfein, the Wood of Leven) they are 'The Whelps of Coel'; in the Welsh Triads, one of the three invincible armies of Britain are the 'Three Hundred Spears of Coel' (three hundred men being a *Gosgordfawr* or war band). So there is plenty of evidence, somewhat scrappy, it is true, for his historic reality and that he was very well known in his time.

It may be that after the Romans departed, tribes well to the south of Hadrian's Wall may have joined Coel's conurbation, extending it to York where he could have left a general, Eluther of the Large Army, to guard these southern territories.

The ancient Welsh genealogies confirm Coel as the chief progenitor of the Men of the North, the *Gwyr Y Gogledd*. There were thirteen principal Men of the North, ten of whom were directly descended from Coel Hen, with the possibility of one other, showing how powerful his Clan was. Even Cunedda Weldig, saviour of the Britons of Cambria (Wales) from early Irish occupation, is descended from Coel Hen, and the following is his family line, taken from the ancient genealogies: Cunedda son of Edyrn, son of Pedwrn or Padarn, son of Gwynnog, son of Coel Hen Godebog.

The North, *Y Gogledd* in this connection, was approximately a line from the mouth of the River Humber to the middle of Cardigan Bay in west Wales, say to the town of Aberdyfi, then north to the Antonine Wall or beyond. If you take the Caledones or Picts to be part of the ancient Britons, since they spoke a Britonic dialect of 'P' Celtic as deduced from present-day place names, especially in the north-east, there should be no reason to exclude them. In fact they were the last remnants of the ancient Britons to practise the particularly British concept of matrilineal succession.

Another important Weldig at about the start of the sixth century, some seventy to one hundred years after Coel's death, at the battle of Coilsfield, was the Chief of the Cornovii, with his main fortress at Wroxeter (Viroconium Cornivorium) in present-day Shropshire, on the north Welsh border with England. This was Vortigern or Vortipor. It is possible that the latter name could be that of one of his sons, who had ambitions to establish himself as High Chief over the surrounding British tribes.

With the help of Saxon mercenaries from the south, he moved east, with conquest in mind. He was opposed by a British war leader, still using a Romano-British name around a century after the Romans had left, Ambrosius Aurelianus. They met in battle just outside Manchester at the Hill of Bowden (pronounced B-awe-Don). This battle was fought around AD 516, and was first reported on by the earliest British historian after the Romans left, St Gildas, who gave it its latinised name Mons Badonicus. (See Chapter 2.) Ambrosius defeated Vortigen and his Saxons, and Vortigen had to flee to the mountains and friendly tribes of north Wales.

The victor, Ambrosius, appears to have gone on a triumphant tour which included a visit to Scotland and Dun Eidin (Edinburgh). This suggests that he, a century after Coel's death, was holding Coel's tribal associations together, i.e., was Northern Dux or Weldig (war leader), and so possibly aroused Vortigen's jealousy.

Ambrosius could be a descendant of Eluther of the Large Army, Coel's general left in York.

A great-great-grandson of Coel, of the Roman tribe the Votadinii or Gotadinii (the Gododdin) was Cunedda, who with his family of eight sons departed Gododdin and moved to Wales, whether by invitation from his southern cousins or for other reasons is not known. He became Weldig and, on finding west Wales overrun by Irish settlers, set about driving them out. In this he was singularly successful particularly in Anglesey and north Wales, and his succeeding dynasty, especially his numerous sons, provided many of the Welsh Chief family progenitors, still quoted to this day as descended from Cunedda, but in reality from Coel Hen Godebog.

It is true that we know who the father of Coel Hen was: Tefgan, but he was a small tribal Chief, and it was his son Coel that the Romans, recognising some special quality, selected and made into an Over or High Chief of a number of clans. They gave him the Roman title Praefectus and thus thrust greatness upon him. He was especially active after their departure, when he had to hold together tribal alliances to prevent incursions from external forces, i.e., the Scoti from Ireland, the Caledones or Picts, and inter-tribal strife – not an easy task, yet one in which he appears to have been successful.

Hector Boece, a much discredited sixteenth century Scottish historian, was well aware of the strong verbal traditions of an ancient 'King' Coel in Ayrshire, but he, as many of the early historians, made his subject much older to show the antiquity of his race, and made him a leader in early or pre-Roman Britain. It is only when Coel is brought forward in time to the fifth century that he fits with others into the correct period.

Yet another grandson of Coel was Caw of Pryden, of Trwcelyn of Cwm Caw(c)lwyd. A rough translation of his name and titles are, Caw of Pryden or Albion, the land between the two walls of the Holly Tower (there is a place, Hollybush on the River Doon in Ayrshire), of the wood of Caw on Clyde. His lands were to be found in Renfrewshire, with an offshoot at the present day estate of Culzean in Ayrshire, which used to be called the 'Lordship of Caw'.

He is accredited with a very large family, one of whom was called Gildas, but like W.F. Skene, the Victorian Historian Royal of Scotland, we do not believe he is the same person as St Gildas, the early historian, owing to the latter's ignorance of anything north of Hadrian's Wall, whereas a Gildas born in Renfrewshire would be familiar with the location. We suspect that this Gildas is Gildas Albanus who settled in Armorica.

Another of Caw's sons was Samson, who it is here suggested trained at St Ninnian's Candida Cassa, to become St Samson, who moved to Wales and then to Armorica, where he became Bishop of Dol.

On his journey from Wales to Armorica, he was accosted by a family who had sickness among their children and beseeched him to heal them. He replied that he did not practise healing but recommended that they sought out, in the forests of the North, the Caledonian Forest, an old man of the woods, famous for his knowledge of herbal medicine, who could help them. *This is a confirmation of Myrddyn (Merlin) in his days as an outcast in the forest of O'Oer.* (See Chapter 10.)

This is why we have taken St Samson to be the son of Caw for his knowledge of northern geography, despite the genealogies giving his father as Amon of Dyfed. This land of the Dementae (Dyfed) seems to have a lot of British names coincidental with the northern tribes!

The family of Caw is very interesting. Firstly, the ancient

genealogies do not confirm his parentage, but we favour him as a grandson of Coel Hen, a son of Ceneu, as another two sons of Ceneu have the same title 'Of Pryden' (i.e. Albion), namely Pabo Post Pryden, and Mar (Maes Gloff) of Pryden, confirming how the descendants of Coel Hen wove a web in the land of Pryden, the land between the two Walls, the land of a future Artur's battles.

A daughter of Caw called Gwenabwy married Llwydeu who was son of Nwython (Nechtan, a northern Brito-Pictish Chief), showing that considerable intermarriage took place between Briton and Caledon or Pict in these far off days.

It is unfortunate that such a giant of his time as Coel Hen appears to have been is only remembered today as a children's nursery rhyme.

This chapter shows the importance of this High Chief to the history of the early Britons, and how his descendants impinged on the story of Artur. Artur through his mother's side is a descendant of 'King' Cole.

It will now be much better appreciated and understood the importance to early history of Old King Cole, Coel Hen Godebog, the Wise and the Splendid, the earliest and most important British or Cumbrian ancestor that we can trace of Artur.

CHAPTER 5

ST GILDAS AND THE
VENERABLE BEDE

Woe, woe to our land, for Rome is no more;
Her legions have left us, and we are alone;
Her galleys are fading away from our shore.
All hope has gone with them. The Eagles have flown.

Edward Shirley

Most of what we know of the early Britons, their tribal names and
territorial locations, we have derived from Roman geographers and
historians, and later, after their departure, by the work of early latinised
Christian scribes.

The earliest of these was **St Gildas**, a sixth-century British monk
who had studied under St Illtud in Wales, but worked somewhere in
south-west England, say around the Severn estuary. He is often
mistaken for Gildas Albanus (of Albion) the son of Caw of Pryden,
who moved to and established himself in Armorica. He wrote a
historical treatise on the southern Britons entitled 'About the Ruin and
Conquest of Britain' (*De Excidio et Conquestu Britanniae*).

Gilda's knowledge of Britain is extremely limited, being confined
to Wales and the south-west of England, and is practically non-existent
about the land and peoples of the east, and more particularly those
north of Hadrian's Wall.

His work is not really a history, although there are obvious historical connotations: for example, he tells that Aetius, Roman Commander of Gaul, failed to respond to an appeal for military help from the Britons when they were being attacked from the sea by the Belgic tribes, who pushed them inland where they were then attacked from the north by the Picts, who pushed them back to the sea. The Roman Eagles, protectors of Britain, had left, never to return.

The work contains chiefly a list of complaints against the Cambrian (Welsh) High Chiefs who, although nominally Christian, did not behave in a Christian-like manner, which was bringing God's wrath down upon them and on the British people in the form of Saxon invasion. He states that, after the first shock of the Saxon invaders, who were cruel plunderers, the British wretches fled from them in all directions, until God gave strength to the survivors under the leadership of one Ambrosius Aurelius or Aurelianus, which name means 'War Leader', whose parents had worn the Roman purple, who began to draw them together. This demonstrates that some of the Roman administrations were still in every-day use, particularly south of the Hadrian Wall.

Under Ambrosius's leadership the Britons regained their strength and challenged the invaders to battle. Sometimes the invaders won and sometimes the Britons. This situation lasted right up to the battle of the siege of Badon Hill. The date of this battle of Badon Hill is still not agreed among historians, but the Cambrian (Welsh) Annals give the date as *c.* AD 516, and since these annals were set down after the time of Bede who introduced AD dates, they are most likely to be accurate.

We start with the Annals' year 1 as AD 445 and from known events in that year and working forward for some seventy-two years, this equates with AD 516, the Annals' date for the battle, and so they are reasonably straightforward to use. It is amazing how many modern historians try to change this dating to an earlier form of Easter Annal date, which can throw it out by some twenty-eight years, *when such datings were abandoned after Bede's history and time.*

Similarly, since Gildas does not mention an Arthur, some find in this proof of Arthur being at Mons Badonicus! The argument is that although Ambrosius becomes the leader of the Britons and has some success against their oppressors, it cannot be assumed he fought in all the battles and that Arthur his deputy fought at the Hill of Badon! It seems more logical to deduce, or assume, that Ambrosius, as their leader, would be expected to do just that and lead in all their battles if possible, especially at a siege, so that if victorious he would bring a period of peace, as indeed there was. These simple deductions for some reason or other are not complicated enough, which seems to be the necessity of deductive reasoning these days.

As with any dates of such an early period one should allow for an error of plus or minus ten years.

According to Gildas the battle was fought in the year of his birth, i.e. AD 516. Again instead of taking the obvious, much is made of other methods of dating to move this date into the fifth century. Gildas was not being obscure, like Nennius later, he simply stated what he knew. These early writers were far too naive to be politically devious.

The battle was between a British Chief, aided by Saxon mercenaries, called by Gildas the 'Superbus Tyrannus'; this was Ambrosius's adversary. To this battle, Gildas gave the latinised name 'Mons Badonicus' (Mount or Hill of Bawdon or Bowden).

The Tyrannus was Gurthrigerno, Vortigern, Vortigen or Vortipor, Chief or Weldig of the Cornovii, a large British tribe centred around present day Wroxeter in Shropshire, close to the north Welsh border. This identification was made later by Nennius.

The ancient stone pillar of Eliseg in Clwyd, Wales, claims Vortigern was son-in-law to Macsen Weldig, Magnus Maximus, Roman Governor of Britain. His opponent Ambrosius was based on York or Elmet, and appears to be carrying the mantle of Old King Coel, i.e.,

Northern Dux, whose High Chieftaincy position probably caused Vortigern's jealousy.

There are difficulties with the time and dates, both of Vortigern and of Ambrosius. They appear to have flourished from early fifth century (*c.* 420) to well into the sixth (*c.* 520)! Phillips and Keatman (*Arthur – The True Story*) put up a good case for their being two Vortigerns, possibly father and son, whilst Dr J. Morris (*The Age of Arthur*) confirms an Ambrosius the elder with his son the younger.

Accepting that there has been a mix-up of datings by these confused generations, and taking the younger of the two generations as the opponents at the battle of Mons Badonicus, the dates can be corrected and confirm that this battle was sixth century, as stated in the Cambrian Annals.

It could be that the earlier Vortigern was of the Dementae tribe, and that the later Vortigern was Chief of the Cornovii, based on Wroxeter. He himself could have had a son Vortipor, making some three Vortigerns in all!

If, as suggested, Vortigern was envious of Ambrosius's High Chieftaincy position, and had he beaten Ambrosius, Vortigern would have been Chief of tribes from the Forth-Clyde line to a line from the Humber to Cardigan Bay. Then he would have turned to the south and exterminated his Saxon allies. He would then have had the same influence as the Romans did at the height of their power, i.e. from the Antonine Wall to the Isle of Wight, so the prize was very great.

Unluckily for Vortigern, Ambrosius completely defeated him. He had to flee to the safety of the north Welsh mountains, which abutted his lands and over which he had some considerable sway. The Saxons dispersed and Ambrosius, either in thanks for help received or in a triumphal tour as a warning to other tribal Chiefs not to attempt the same ploy, appears to have visited southern Scotland, even perhaps Edinburgh, Dun Eidin, where, according to Professor Goodrich, he founded Holyrood Abbey.

If, as we argue, Ambrosius was Northern Dux and this was the reason for Vortigern's attempted usurpation, it would confirm that Coel Hen's overlordship in the north, after the Romans had left, was still being held together.

Gildas tells us he is writing his history in his forty-fourth year, so if he was born in the year of Mons Badonicus, *c.* AD 516, he would be writing around AD 560 and well into the second half of the sixth century – Artur's century. If a person called Artur had been living in Gilda's Britain, the lands south of Hadrian's Wall, fighting battles and winning them against invading Angles or Saxons, or Jutes or Frisians, or any others, then there is no doubt that Gildas would have mentioned him. Yet there is not a whisper of any such person in his writings; even if Arthur had been a fifth century person, Gildas would surely have included him in his story.

Why then is Gildas so silent? Was it because, as he sat writing his story in his forty-fourth year, unbeknown to him, north of Hadrian's Wall, a war leader called Artur was indeed engaged in fighting and winning battles against invaders, the Inglis or Northumbrians with some Jutish or Saxon support?

This particular group included Eocha and Ebissa with their descendants. Eocha, having later to leave the north and return to Kent, according to the *Anglo-Saxon Chronicles*, landed on the upper reaches of the river Forth, just north of the Antonine Wall. This was in the district of Calatria or Calathros (possibly Catreath). After some time and considerable reinforcements, he moved aggressively to the west, forcing an Artur in these lands to intervene.

Look at any Scottish telephone directory under the letter 'I' and see the large number of Inglis names, descendants of the Inglis or Northumbrians who invaded Scotland, then known as Albion, and notice the places called Ingliston, towns of the Inglis, all extant to this day, and all of course well and truly 'Scotticised' by now.

Of all this, Gildas was completely ignorant, hence his total silence on the matter. It is doubtful if Gildas even realised that the peoples beyond the Wall were Christians, and Christianised well before him. They would be barbarians to him!

However, Gildas does give us some insights and hints where to look. The main purpose of his book was to take to task several British Chiefs with tribal lands all south of Hadrian's Wall, principally in Wales and the south-west.

He castigates them for their Christian backsliding, inter-tribal warfare and neglect of agriculture causing great famine, so much so that the Picts stopped raiding, and in particular wasting time drinking and listening to bardic songs and epic poems. He little realised that the newest songs and poems were heralding in a new Heroic Age – the age of the Men of the North – the *Gwyr Y Gogledd*, among whose exploits were included those of an Artur, in the form of a minor Saga.

It is this cornucopia of song and poem telling us of the great battle of Arftyrydd, of the heroic defeat of Catreath, of the prowess of Urien and his son Owain and, of course, Artur and his twelve battles, that we have to turn to for historical confirmation. It was the twelve battles that made his name – he appears to have fought them all in one single fighting season i.e., during spring and summer, a most unusual feat of arms and of military logistics. Gildas was ignorant of all this, and so his history, bereft of happenings north of the wall, is, unhappily, of little value in relation to a historic Artur.

There are some differing versions of Gildas's life. One is that he is Gildas son of Caw of Pryden, whose lands were in Renfrewshire, Strathclyde, but like W.F. Skene we reject this. His name is associated with Clyde or Clwyd, and because of his ignorance of peoples and places north of Hadrian's Wall, we place his birth in Clwyd in north Wales and not on the Clyde in Renfrewshire, which would explain his knowledge of the Chiefs in Wales and the south-west.

We must now look at Gildas's story of the battle of Mons Badonicus or Badonis, a latinised version of a British placename, Badon, Bawdon or Bowden Hill, and give our preferred location for it: the Hill of Bowden (old pronunciation Bawdon) just south of Manchester, near Altringham.

Firstly: because it is on the eastern edge of the main Cornovii territory, that is to say, Vortigern's lands, and on the borders of Ambrosius's tribal conglomerate's western boundary.

Secondly: when defeated, Vortigern flees to the mountains of north Wales, whereas if this battle had taken place around Bath, as is often suggested, he would have had to flee to the mountains of south Wales. There he would not have had a lot of influence.

Thirdly: some three hundred years later, when Nennius describes Arthur's twelve battles from his epic poem, he finds that Arthur's last battle is at a British Hill of Badon, Bawdon or Bowden, which he equates with Gildas's Hill of Bowden and describes wrongly as Gildas's latinised Mons Badonicus. This was Ambrosius's battle, and *not* Artur's. A quirk of nomenclature gave two British geographical locations, the Hills of Bowden, some two hundred miles apart, exactly the same British name, and thus caused years of confusion. Ambrosius's battle was fought some forty-odd years earlier than Artur's Hill of Bowden, which was in the plain of Slamannan, just south of Camelon in Falkirk, Stirlingshire.

Indeed there are numerous ancient Bowden place names still to be found in Britain!

It is therefore believed that Bowden was pronounced in those days with the 'o' short as in 'Boffin', i.e. 'Bawdon' and by verbal transcription became Gildas's 'Badon', the 'a' here pronounced as in 'ball' – Bawdon, i.e. Ba'don, a transcriptional loss of the letter w, before being latinised from Bowden to Bawdon to Badon.

It is hoped to show instances where, when verbal traditions come to be written down, single letters get lost or are misplaced, but when they are retrieved, a whole new meaning is put into their understanding. (See Excalibur in Chapter 9.)

Because Gildas's writings are a cleric's warning of disasters to come if the present nominally Christian Chiefs do not amend their ways, foretelling that disaster will surely befall the British people, he has acquired the nickname of 'British Jeremiah'.

> *They taught us to labour, to build, and to plough,*
> *To fashion the clay and to quarry the stone,*
> *Vain, vain all our learning to succour us now*
> *The foe is upon us. The Eagles have flown.*

E. Shirley

The Venerable Bede is the first true historian of the English peoples. He was a monk at the joint monastery of Monkwearmouth and Jarrow where, at the very early age of seven years, he was taken into the Church of Northumbria to be cared for and brought up in Christianity.

Born in AD 673, he became a monk, a gentle, humble and pious scholar, the greatest in Saxon England. His *Ecclesiastical History of the English Nation* is the chief source of early history for the period. He died in AD 735.

His work impinges on nearly all matters, including Irish, Scottish, Pictish and British (Welsh), as they affected their relationship with the English, and in particular the Northumbrians.

The Northumbrian Church, despite the Synod of Whitby making it nominally under the Roman Church, remained for many years essentially Celtic, owing to King Oswald who had fled to Iona from the successful attack by the Welsh in AD 632.

When Oswald returned as a Christian of the Ionaian Church, he brought with him the humble St Aidan, to preach in his land. They travelled together, Aidan preaching in Gaelic with Oswald translating into Saxon English. He gave the island of Lindisfarne to St Aidan.

Earlier, according to Bede, Run or Rhun, son of Urien of Rheged, helped in the Christianising of the Northanhymbres or Northumbrians, or sometimes the 'Ambrones', this last name suggesting the people from the land of Ambrosius!! Rhun, one would assume, would have been trained at Candida Cassa under the disciples of St Ninnian in his father's land of Rheged. In c. AD 627, he baptised Edwin King of Northumbria and many of his people; he was known then as Archbishop Paulinius of York.

St Aidan set up his mission on the isle of Lindisfarne, and the Northumbrian Church was run from there.

For the earliest history Bede relies chiefly on St Gildas, who of course did not mention an Arthur; *likewise neither does Bede!*

Bede, with his knowledge of the early Northumbrian Church and its surprisingly close relations with the Columban Church on Iona, must have had knowledge of St Adamnan's *Life of Columba,* and know that Aidan Mac Gabhran had a son named Artur, but he did not realise that this person could be a historic candidate for a legendary Artur. This might be because at his time there were *no* folk tales around about an Arthur, and that these stories had to await the revelations by Nennius in the ninth century. Then, for the next three hundred years, legends began to build up, culminating in Geoffrey of Monmouth's book in the twelfth century, the basis for the later fables.

One can say the same about the Venerable Bede as about Gildas. If there had been knowledge of a great British King Hero called Arthur in his historical time, he would most certainly have mentioned him. Their silence speaks loud and clear, *Artur was a minor war leader in the lesser known north,* whose exploits, remembered in ancient Bardic verse, got lost, and had to await the rediscovery by Nennius in the early ninth century.

CHAPTER 6
COLUMCILLE OR ST COLUMBA,
1ST ABBOT OF IONA

A youth shall be born out of the north
With the rising of the nations;
Ireland shall be made fruitful by the great flame,
And Alba, friendly to him.

Mochta of Lugbad

St Columba, or Columcille to give him his Iro-Scots name, was born around Gartan Lough in County Down, Ireland, in *c.* AD 521. His father was Fedilmith son of Fergus of Cenel (Clan) Conail, a royal line of the Ui Neil. His mother was Ethne or Eithne daughter of Mac Naue, a King of the Cenel Gulban.

He was therefore of noble birth, and like all the sons of such was fostered out to be educated. This was at the hands of a Presbyter called Criuthnechan, son of Cellachan. This priest's name suggests that he was of the Cruithne, the Picts of Ireland, who appear to differ from other Irishmen only in that they spoke a dialect of Brythonic or 'P' Celtic. They later became known in Ulster or *Ulad* as the tribe of Dal nAraide.

Cruithnechan was apparently trained at Candida Cassa by St Ninnian, who possibly founded the very first monastic school (or Bangor) in Ireland at Aondrium on Mahee Isle, Strangford Loch. This tutoring by a British speaking monk possibly gave Columcille his penchant for dealing with the Picts or Caledones of Scotland in his later evangelising years, spending some nine years, on and off, among these northern tribes.

After his period of foster education, Columcille decided to go in for the Church, a not so surprising decision, as this new religious philosophy was sweeping the country under the impetus of St Patrick and others, offering new opportunities not only of bringing the word of the Bible to the many, but religious and political power.

He entered the monastic school of St Finnian of Molvile, an Irish Pictish Abbot, who had trained at St Ninnian's Candida Cassa. Columcille was ordained priest by Bishop Echten, and set about founding a number of monastic houses. He is credited with a great number.

It appears at this time, that he borrowed from St Finnian of Molvile a famous book or psalter, Jerome's translations of the Psalms, and immediately set about copying it. On this being discovered he was accused of stealing (breach of copyright). The dispute was very heated, and was eventually taken to the High King Diarmit for him to resolve.

Diarmit, with Solomon-like wisdom, made his famous pronouncement: 'To every cow its calf, and to every book its small book (copy)'.

Hence Columcille lost his case. In great anger he roused his Clan to war and vengeance, bringing his adversaries to battle at Culdrevny. He carried the day with great slaughter, as it was claimed three thousand of his accusers were slain.

This ferocity shocked the general populace. A synod was set up to judge him and pronounced that he should be exiled. Columcille accepted the judgement, but took his time in carrying it out. He took two years after this judgement to leave Northern Ireland with twelve companions and journey to the new colony of Dalriada, on the west coast of Scotland. He landed at Kintyre.

When Columcille arrived in Kintyre, he was met by his cousin Conail, fifth King of Dalriada. Conail made him welcome, and granted him title to the Island of Iona to set up a Christian mission.

The Venerable Bede states that St Columba had also to get permission of the Over or High King, Brude of the Caledones or Picts. Whatever the rights of this, St Columba, now giving him his sanctified name, did set up his ministry on Iona, and it became the prime religious institution in Britain and Ireland for the next three hundred years, until the Viking invasions of the ninth century brought about its demise.

During this period there was a time when the fortunes of the Scots of Dalriada were at a very low ebb. They had fallen foul of their Pictish overlords and lost a number of battles against them, so that it looked as if they would be overwhelmed. In this circumstance, they moved what is called today the 'Iona Chronicle' to the safety of Bangor in Northern Ireland. This Chronicle formed the basis of the Scottish and North British references in the many Irish Annals. (See *Studies in the History of Dalriada* by Dr John Bannerman.)

St Columba, having established his mission on Iona, proceeded with his evangelical work among the Picts or Caledones of the north, visiting the High Chief Brude or Bredi at Craig Phadrig, Inverness.

Brude is an interesting person as he is accredited as being the son of Maelgwyn Gwynedd, and as there is no record of the tribes of Gwynedd going to war with the northern Picts, this would appear to be another case of matrilineal succession. Here a son of Gwynedd moved many miles to the north, to seek out and marry a woman of title, indeed he became a High Chief.

In this evangelical work, Columba was supported by Conail.

There is no evidence that St Columba ever, on his travels on the mainland of Scotland, ventured south of Hadrian's Wall. Indeed, the furthest south that he is reported to have been, on mainland Scotland excluding Kintyre, is Glasgow, where he met St Kentigern (St Mungo) and exchanged crosiers. He may also have obtained the services of two of the followers of Kentigern, to act as translators of the dialect of the northern Picts, which was 'P' Celtic. The Irish Picts or Cruithne St Comgal and St Cainnech did this duty.

This poses a question: Geoffrey of Monmouth claims that St Columba officiated at Artur's coronation, somewhere in England or Wales, countries that there is no evidence that he ever visited. There is something wrong with Geoffrey's reporting, and an explanation is offered later.

St Columba's close relationship with Conail the King gave him political influence, and when Conail died apparently without heir, he was looked to to proclaim and ordain the next King. Conail's uncle Gabhran had been the fourth King, and Gabhran's sons now came into the reckoning for succession, as Dunchad, Conail's eldest son and others had been killed at the battle of Delgu, *c.* 574, in Kintyre. Gabhran's eldest son Eoganin was expected as the eldest to take up the office. Columba, however, had other ideas.

Gabhran in his youth had spent considerable time through in the east, on the upper reaches of the River Forth, where he met and married Lluan, a woman of the Britons. Their first son Eoganin was therefore half Iro-Scots and half British. The same deduction should have applied to Aidan their second son, but there were rumours.

The *Yellow Book of Lecan* tells the story of a family from Ireland, Eochaid and his wife Feidelm, who have to flee the land and who are given refuge in Dalriada by Gabhran in his eastern estates through on the River Forth. The wife of the escapers is pregnant, and comes into labour at the same time as Lluan, Gabhran's wife. They share the same labour room and, as fortune would have it, their births occur on the same night, Lluan being delivered of twin girls and her companion Feidlem of twin boys, later named Brandub and Aidan. The two women agree to swop a girl for a boy so that they have one of each sex. Everyone is sworn to secrecy, but this proves impossible and the rumour is that Aidan is an exchangeling, that he is not the true son of Gabhran. *It is a very unlikely story!*

St Columba, who is about to perform the first Christian ordination of a King of Dalriada, and is planning to do so with some great ceremony for that time, would like his nominee to be pure Iro-Scots. He is aware that this is not the case with Eoganin, the eldest son, but because of the rumours surrounding the birth of Aidan, there is a possibility, and only a slight possibility, that he could be a true Irishman.

He is in a quandary. The populace expects him to declare for Eoganin, the elder. He comes up with the ideal solution, one that he was to use frequently in his lifetime. He declares he has visions when Angels of God appear to him, one with a glass book, and reveal to him God's wishes. Who can gainsay God!

So he has a number of visions and proclaims Aidan as God's choice, a stance that not even Eoganin could object to. Thus did Aidan become the sixth King of Dalriada.

As suggested earlier, Columba made a great religious ceremony of Aidan's coronation. Nothing like it had ever been seen before as far as the local tribes and peoples were concerned. Neighbouring Chiefs, petty Kings and over Kings were all invited to witness the ordination, including of course Aidan's own children, among whom was his son Artur.

A report describes Aidan's coronation by St Columba at which Artur was present. It is written in Irish Gaelic, a language that Geoffrey of Monmouth is not acquainted with, and in which he recognises only a few words, mainly 'St Columba', 'coronation' or 'crowning' and 'Artur', as well as some well known Chiefs' names who were guests. This leads him to the wrong conclusion that it is a description of Arthur's crowning.

After becoming King, Aidan and Columba did not appear to get on very well. Aidan summoned a large number of Druids to put St

Columba to the test, and they engaged in a number of debates, but Columba routed his opponents, and remained Abbot and political advisor to Dalriada. He even accompanied Aidan to the important Convention of Drumcett in *c.* AD 575.

The ease with which Druids were summoned, and so many of them, somewhere between twenty-seven and forty-seven, must pose the question: was this philosophy still being practised in parts of Dalriada alongside Christianity? Or had Aidan's association with Myrddin, Chief Druid of the Selgovae tribe, at the battle of Arftyrydd, caused him to have doubts about his Christian upbringing, giving him a motive to invite Druids to his Kingdom? It is an interesting question.

St Adamnan, in his life of St Columba, written some ninety odd years after the Saint's death and so almost within living memory, tells of a conversation between Aidan and Columba. St Columba asks him which of his sons does he think will succeed him? Aidan answers either his eldest son Eochaid Find or his second eldest Artur. Columba disagrees and instructs Aidan to send for the remainder of his children, foretelling that the one who, when he enters, climbs on to his knee and hugs him will succeed Aidan.

This is done, and one of the younger children does sit on the Saint's knee and hug him. This is Eochad Bude (Eocho Bui), who does indeed become the seventh King after his father.

According to St Adamnan, Artur son of Aidan was killed at the battle of the Miathi, along with his elder brother Eochaid Find. This name equates with the Roman tribe of the Maetae, who were located on the upper reaches of the River Forth, around present-day Clackmannan.

This battle in *c.* 582, was also subject to another of Columba's visions, in which he declared Aidan the victor but with sorrow as his two eldest sons were killed.

Here Columba's interpretation or vision would appear to be wrong: it was not a great victory but a defeat. For a victor, Aidan did not sustain the field for very long, and had to return and fight the battle of Slamannan (Mannan) a year or so later (*c.* 583), to recover his wife's estates and avenge the death of his sons.

The battle of the Miathi or Maetae, we equate with the battle of Camlan, a corruption of Camelon or Carron, the battle of *Camlan Guotadin* in the land of the Gotadinii or Gododdin in the north. It was fought on the River Carron, close to Camelon. Skene called it the battle of Kir Kin, which looks like the spelling used in the Annals of Ulster, Strathcairrin being an old spelling of the River Carron, mainly Cairrin – Cair Rin – Kir Kin. An explanation for the battle's occurrence is given later, with Aidan's return eventually to redress the situation.

Dr Bannerman, however, in his book *Studies in the History of Dalriada*, is convincing that Kir Kin is a separate and later battle at the Pictish capital of Fortren (Cercen – Ker ken), when Brude son of Maelgwyn is killed, and this is accepted as the most likely explanation of Skene's battle.

It is not known whether Artur and his elder brother were buried on or near the battlefield, or whether Aidan took their bodies back with him to be buried on Iona with the blessing of Columba. The latter course is very likely.

Adamnan tells us of another of Columba's predictions, at the time of Aidan's ordination. Columba warns Aidan that he and his heirs will continue in kingship as long as neither he nor his descendants ever do ill to Columba's clan. His words are: 'Believe me, O Aidan, that none of thy enemies shall be able to oppose thee, until you first work deceit upon me and my successors. Wherefore direct thou thy children to commend to their children, their grandchildren, and their prosperity, not to let the sceptre pass out of their hands through evil counsels.'

This prophecy apparently came true when Aidan's grandson Domnal Brec, Dyfnwal Vrych in Britonic, got involved in the battle of Mag Rath or Roth against the descendants of Columba. Domnal Brec was killed a few years later fighting against the Britons of Strathclyde, and so ended Aidan's line in the Kingship of Dalriada, as foretold by Columba.

Doubt has been thrown on this story by recent historians, who feel Domnal Brec was not involved in this battle, and that this interpretation has been inserted to make it fit Columba's prediction. (See *Studies in the History of Dalriada* by Dr John Bannerman.)

Mention has been made of the Convention of Drumcett, where Columba accompanied Aidan, as his advisor, to a conference of Kings. Here he played his part in securing the release of Dalriada from being a colony of Irish Dalriata, to become a separate Kingdom in its own right, as well as negotiating his own restitution back in the Irish Church. Aidan had to agree to assist Dalriata by 'hostings' and other expeditions when called upon.

St Columba, of Royal birth, imperious, brave but terrible in wrath, a personality who commanded the attention of all, be they king or beggar, although a man of God had a lively and effective influence in politics, particularly in Dalriadan affairs. He was quick tempered and politically ambitious, an enigmatic personality, but of great stature, living at the time of St Gildas, who pales into insignificance beside him. He was a maker of Kings, and responsible for Artur's Christian upbringing, yet was overlooked by later historians, when much of the history of the Northern Britons or Cymry is in the Irish Annals, and Columcille's in St Adomnan's life of this Saint.

CHAPTER 7

AIDAN MAC GABHRAN, 6TH KING OF DALRIADA

I have been in the place where Gwendolen was slain,
The son of Ceidaw, the pillar of song,
Where the ravens screamed over blood.

Black Book of Carmarthen

The above lines, describing Gwyn ap Nudd, could equally apply to Aidan, King of the Dalriadic Scots, who was a most important figure of the sixth century. His family roots were in Dalriata in Northern Ireland, and it will be useful to go back in time to attempt a historical background to his eventual relationships with the Britons, the Caledones or Picts, and with the Northumbrians.

About the year AD 500, the Romans having long departed, the situation south of the Antonine Wall was much disturbed. The Britons who had been greatly affected by the Roman occupation were rather more peaceful than those, the Caledonians or Picts, north of the Antonine Wall, and it is certain that considerable pressure from north to south existed.

Into this situation prior to AD 500 there were frequent incursions from Ireland by the Scoti into the Western Isles, but around AD 500, instead of returning to Ireland with their booty, they formed a small colony in Kintyre, which became known as Dal-Riada as distinct from their Irish land, known as Dal-Riata.

To many, the colonisation of Dalriada seems strange, since it was carried out apparently unopposed by the indigenous population. Fergus son of Ercc, King in Dalriata, moved his seat from Northern Ireland to Dalriada, soon after a stable situation had been achieved, without any apparent fear or resentment from the local inhabitants.

It must of course be borne in mind that the Scots (Irish) had, over a long period of time, been in the habit of raiding the western seaboard of Scotland, and indeed Britain, and no doubt mixed families would occur. There would also be doubt about each other's strength: the Scots fearing the Caledones or Picts and vice versa. The original invading number of people being only about 150, it would therefore be in the interests of the Scots to aim for a peaceful penetration.

Eventually, as they grew stronger, friction did occur and many battles then took place.

There is however another possible explanation which we can consider by reverting back to the fourth century, to the time of the Three Collas: Colla Uais, Colla Dacroich and Colla Meann, the sons of Eochaidh Dubhlain who were expelled from Ireland by Muireadhach Tireach around AD 326.

One, Colla Uais, fled to Alba (Albion, now Scotland), where he married the Chieftainess of an Alban tribe, thus forming family relationships between the Albans and the Irish, which also introduced a small population of 'Q' speaking Celts into Albion. The Collas are described as 'A Quo Airthir and Ui Cremthan', suggesting that they and the Irish are the ancestors of Artur via the Cremthan, but the Cremthan are of the Dessi tribe, that settled in Dyfed in south Wales, where an Arthur of Dyfed, their descendant in the late sixth century, was often mixed up with Artur of the north. (See *The Figure of Arthur* by Dr Richard Barber.)

Colla Uais had four sons and the eldest Eochaid, from whom it is claimed comes Somerled, Lord of the Isles and Clan Donald.

Nath I mac Fiachrach, victor over Coel Hen in the fifth century, was descended from the Collas.

Further proof may exist by looking back to the Roman occupation, whose geographers made several censuses of the tribes of Britain. Those tribes north of the Antonine Wall were given the general name Caledones and remained so until their later censuses before leaving Britain, when they named a people north of the Antonine Wall as the Dicaledones, the divided or split Caledones. In other words, they had distinguished a new tribe who did not speak a Brythonic or 'P' Celtic dialect, and were different, hence the change in name.

This suggestion may explain how the Scots of Dalriada originally had an easy and successful settlement on the west coast. They had settled among a people of a somewhat similar culture, who spoke a dialect similar to their own, which may well have influenced their choice of landing site, the descendants of Colla Uais.

Ercc, King of Dalriata in Northern Ireland, had three sons, who settled Dalriada, Loarn, Angus, and Fergus. Loarn settled in Lorne, Angus occupied Islay and Jura, whilst Fergus settled in Bute, Arran, and Knapdale, with his son Comgal taking Cowal.

This seems to be the generally accepted brief view of the history of the colonisation. Dr John Bannerman, however, in his book *Studies of the History of Dalriada*, suggests that they were not brothers, that the original founding was the work of Angus and Loarn and that Fergus, who had succeeded his father Ercc as King of Irish Dalriata, is said, under pressure from the Southern Irish, to have moved his seat of authority to Scottish Dalriada, the object being to ensure his sovereignty over these new lands and so become the first King.

Fergus died in the third year of the colony, then under tribute to Nial Mac Aed in northern Ireland, as well as to the Picts of Alba, a matter which was to cause trouble in time to come.

The development of power in Dalriada on the death of Fergus passed to his son Domgart or Domangart, who in turn was succeeded by his elder son Comgal, and he was followed by his younger brother Gabhran as fourth King in Dalriada, whose rule was somewhat turbulent.

It is important, here, to realise that Gabhran spent some of his earlier years in the eastern part of the country, namely in the area around the upper reaches of the River Forth, i.e., at Snawdoun, ancient name for Stirling, in the tribal land of Mannau Gododdin, the Mannaw of the North.

Here he met and married Lluan, a British woman, daughter of Brychan of Brechiniog from south Wales, who had, along with other members of her family, moved to southern Scotland. It is possible that their early children were born in this area, thus introducing British blood into the royal line of Dalriada. This is according to the British document 'Cognatio Brychan'.

Again, the early British documents 'De Situ Brychaniauc and Cognatio Brychan' record the marriages to northern Nobles of Brychan's daughters, besides Lluan Gabhran's wife; Nyfain became wife to Cynfarch O'Oer of the Selgovae, mother of Urien and Loth; Gwawr became wife to Elidir Lydanwyn, Cynfarch's brother, and mother to Llywarch Hen; Nefydd wife to Tudwal, a Saint at Llech Celyddon in the north; whilst Gwrgon Goddeu, possibly of Cadzow (Goddeu), was wife of Cadrod Calchyyndd – these and many others of his family were located in Mannia or Mannau Gododdin, with the town of Brechin (Brechiniog of the north) remembering the family name to this day.

Brychan himself is said to be buried at an island of Enys Brachan, near Mannia in the north.

Another matter which may have had an effect on this union, going back into the history of the three Collas: they had been forced to leave Ireland by being beaten in battle by Muireadhach Tireach and one took refuge in Alba. This was Colla Uais, who obtained extensive lands by marrying Oileach, daughter of the 'King' of Alba. It could be it was through this connection that Gabhran would have had land interests in Mannau Gododdin. Certainly he and his descendants paid a great deal of attention to that district and fought a number of battles in its neighbourhood which would also be sufficient reason for Gabhran's son Aidan's attention.

Gabhran was killed at a battle against the Picts *c.* AD 558/560, or died at least shortly after the battle, probably from wounds received, against Brude Mac Maelcon, King of Picts, with his fortress at Craig Phadrig, Inverness.

Brude was son of Maelgwyn of Gwynedd and suggests another example of matrilineal succession, this time by a Briton from Gwynedd going to the far north, seeking a woman with rights to tribal lands, where he becomes an Over or High Chief. He was killed at the battle of Kir Kin or Cer Cen, the Pictish capital of Fortren, in *c.* AD 569, at the hands of Aidan Mac Gabhran, whose son Domangart was also killed there.

Conaill Mac Comgall, Gabhran's nephew, now ruled in Dalriada, but was regarded as a lesser ruler by the powerful Caledones, and his reign was of short duration.

Columba in *c.* AD 563 was exiled from Ireland, and was welcomed by his cousin Conaill to Dalriada, to be later settled in Iona by permission of the Picts, according to the Venerable Bede. Conail died *c.* AD 574, but his eldest son Dunchad and others, including Nechtan and Artan (pure Pictish names, the latter probably the Pictish form for Artur), had been killed at the battle of Delgu, in Kintyre, in AD 574.

Aidan, son of Gabhran, under the sponsorship of St Columba, succeeded to the Kingship. Thus entered one of the most powerful leaders of Dalriada, and a military leader ahead of his time, on to the stage of history. His particular interest here was for both land ownership and military expansion, also the coming threat of the Northumbrians moving north along the east coast from Bernicia.

However, the Scots of Dalriada were able to rely upon the assistance of the Irish; thus there was a background of reserves giving the Scots a sense of power which they tended to overestimate, for instance with Gabhran's defeat by the Picts in c. 558/60.

It will be remembered that the original Dalriadan colony was subject to tribute to the Irish High King as well as to the Pictish King. This was a substantial burden upon the people of Dalriada, and with the powerful support of St Columba a convention at Drumclett was arranged between the Irish King Aed Mac Ainmuir and Aidan.

The real purpose of this convention was aimed at relieving Aidan from restrictions upon his ability to act militarily on his own account, to relieve his people from paying Irish tribute. Meanwhile St Columba, having been exiled out of Ireland, sought reinstatement into the Irish Church, with power to act on religious matters in Dalriada and Alba. Many other matters in the relationship were settled, such as that Dalriada would become a separate Kingdom under Aidan, while Dalriata was to remain subject to King Aed. There were however some drawbacks. Aidan could no longer call on fighting men from Dalriada in times of trouble. Suffice to say, this turned out to be an easy-going arrangement and in later years he did get help from Ireland, so the arrangement worked amicably in both directions.

Aidan, now free to act as King in his own right, being a restless and ambitious character began to examine the extent of his Kingdom. His father, Gabhran, had spent much time in the upper Forth region around Snawdoun (the old name for Stirling). There he met and married a woman of the Britons, Lluan, daughter of Brychan, a Chief of the Dementae tribe, Aidan's mother. Aidan followed suit and in his youth did the same, and during his sojourn in the east, met and married Creirwy, daughter of Clydno Eidyn, Artur's mother, of whom little is known other than what can be gleaned from the old Welsh tracts: the

Bonneds (the Lives). She was a sister to one of Urien of Rheged's wives.

These tracts tell us that Urien had at least three wives, two of whom the ancient genealogies show as having a sister, Ethni and Denu. It also names their husbands, and neither is Aidan. His third wife was Euronwy, daughter of Clydno Eidyn, and there are three names given in association with her: Euronwy, Eurnaid, and Creirwy. The first two both begin with 'Eur' but the endings are different: '-wy' is a very common Britonic ending and the other ending '-naid' is common to the Britons, the Caledones or Picts, and even the Irish or Scots, and could be used in preference in a Northern dialect. Hence it can be accepted that Euronwy and Eurnaid are one and the same, but when one looks at Creirwy, there is no similarity in the names apart from the common British ending '-wy', and one can find no real reason why the early translators claimed all three were one and the same. Creirwy is therefore considered sister to Euronwy, wife of Urien, and is here offered as the most likely candidate to be wife of Aidan Mac Gabhran. Her father Clydno Eidyn was one of the thirteen Heroic Men of the North, the *Gwyr Y Gogledd*, and is recognised as one of the most important Chiefs in Mannu Gododdin.

Because of the way his name is spelt, it would appear reasonable to equate him with Caer Eidyn which is mostly spelt with a 'y' where Dinas Eidin or Dun Eidin (Edinburgh) is most often spelt with an 'i'. Caer Eidyn has been identified as being Carriden, adjoining Bo'ness (Borrowstounness) on the banks of the River Forth on the plain of Slamannan in Stirlingshire.

Whatever the relationship of Aidan's wife to other tribes, it is reasonably certain that she was of British or Brito-Pictish stock and most likely sister to Urien's wife. The children of this marriage would be three-quarters Britonic, and since Aidan himself was half British, their children rapidly became more and more identified with the major interests of the Britons, located between the two walls, and as such, their exploits were getting mentioned in the verses of the British bards.

Furthermore, Creirwy, as daughter of an important Chief, because of matrilineal succession held title to the lands of Camelon and Avolond. Camelon is the district in Falkirk named after the Roman fort of that name, just north of the Antonine Wall. We suspect that the local tribes took possession of it, on it being abandoned by the Romans, as an ideal Chief's Hall, while Avolond is suggested as the area of land or estate lying between the rivers Avon and Almond, both of which are in the plain of Slamannan. Creirwy passed the lairdship of her birthright to her husband Aidan.

It will be remembered that Aidan, not being Gabhran's eldest son and natural successor, originally had no expectation of the Kingship of Dalriada, that being the presumption of his elder brother Eoganin. His marriage of course brought him property which forced him into the political life of southern Scotland. i.e., the Britonic tribes between the two walls.

His wife's cousin, Gwendalleau, became Chief of the Selgovae by virtue of his marriage to the widow of Merchion Gul, through matrilineal succession, so Aidan became more and more involved with the affairs of the Britons. This marriage of Gwendalleau into the Chieftaincy of the Selgovae, however, does not appear to have met with the approval of Meirchion Gul's children, namely Cynfarch O'Oer and two of his powerful sons, Urien of Rheged and Low or Loth (Llew or Lleu in Welsh) of Orkney and Lothian.

Aidan's daughter Gwyar married Loth of Lothian and this now placed him in the position of being related to two of the very powerful British families in this central area, Cydno Eidyn of Slamannan and Cynfarch O'Oer of the Selgovae, including his two powerful sons Urien of Rheged and Loth of Lothian.

It will not now be difficult to imagine the turmoil into which these tribes were advancing. The Northern Caledones or Picts were pressing southwards, the Dalriadans were forcing their way to their lands in Slamannan and the estuaries of the rivers Carron and Forth, while the Angles or Inglis were coming up from Bambro and Bernicia in the south, leaving the Britons between the walls to be attacked from all directions.

Aidan, regarded as one of the most competent military commanders of his time, was becoming very much concerned about the general advance of the Inglis or Angles, northwards along the eastern coastline. His eldest sons, Eochaid Find, Artur and Domangart were naturally involved in the general disturbances, which had been developing ever since the withdrawal of the Romans first from the Antonine Wall and then from the Wall of Hadrian.

In those times of death in battle, it seemed to be customary to proclaim your successor well in advance, therefore when the question of Aidan's successor was raised, St Columba chose Eocho Buide, saying, 'none of these three will be ruler, for they will fall in battle, slain by enemies.'

At this time, the relationship between the clans and their families, especially those directly to be involved with Aidan and his family, is relevant, though somewhat complicated.

We start with Morken, Chief of the Alcluyd Britons, whose capital was at Dunbreton (Dun of the Britons or Alcluyd, now Dumbarton Rock). He was attacked and deposed by his nephew Ryderych Hael and sought sanctuary from Gwendalleau, Chief of the Selgovae, who accepted Ryderych's conquest and moved Morken to the safety of his southern fortress, Caer Gwendalleau, at present day Carwinnley, among the knowles (hills) of Arthuret (Arftyrydd) east of Carlisle.

This move was apparently unacceptable to Ryderych and he planned revenge. Having this in mind he formed an alliance with Eliffer Gosgordfawr of Elmet. There were difficulties in the relationship between the family of Elmet and that of Cynfarch O'Oer of the Selgovae. Eliffer had married a daughter of Cynfarch O'Oer with whom he had a son, Arthur. Despite this he set her aside and took another wife, Madrun, by whom he had two sons, Peredur (killed at the battle of Caer Greu by Eda, 'Big Knees') and Gwrgi.

Ryderych formed another part of the alliance with Dinogad of Powys, probably a son or relative of Maelgwyn of Gwynedd, which was, on the face of it, an unusual choice, there being no obvious reason for Dinogad/Maelgwyn to become involved. Perhaps there was some personal animosity between Powys and Gwendalleau, or Dinogad was in some way under an obligation to Ryderych.

When the battle of Arftyrydd did start, some weeks passed before the men of Powys arrived on the scene. It is often suggested that this was an evangelical war, a Christian alliance, against the last Druid tribe in southern Scotland, the Selgovae. This appears to us be a wrong view. If Ryderych had wished to attack the Selgovae as a tribe, he would have done so in the north whilst his two allies would have attacked from the south, thus squeezing the Selgovae in a pincer movement. His actions speak louder than words: his army tip-toes out of Alcluyd, slips past the whole western side of the Selgovae territory without alarming them, and creeps across Rheged, not upsetting Urien, and gets into northern England to meet up with his allies. His sole intention is to attack the sanctuary where Morken is known to be.

Elliffer's two sons, Peredur (note this Peredur is not the Peredur of Dun Pedler in Lothian of the Gotadini, killed at Cathreath) and Gwrgi are waiting for him, supported by Dunawt the Stout (hearted), the son of Cynan Garwyn, son of Brochwell Ysgithrog (there could be some doubt about this Dunawd, as a son of Cynan Garwyn would appear to be rather young to be at this battle), and Cynfelyn the Leperous, probably the son of Bleidudd.

They await the arrival of Dinogad of Powys; he does not appear and they decide to start the action without him. They turn north and attack Arftyrydd (Arthuret, Arturet or anciently Artruth) with the sole intention of attacking Morken in Gwendalleau's sanctuary.

Aidan, though a Christian brought up under the influence of St Columba, finds himself obliged to support his British family, no doubt at his wife's behest, and with the help of Dreon or Dingad son of Nudd, and possibly his brother Gwyn, hurries to Arftyrydd in support of Gwendalleau.

So started one of the greatest battles of the sixth century, which was so drawn out that it lasted two and a half months. It was fought over land just north-east of Carlisle. It was great in that after two weeks the Chief Gwendalleau was killed, but the defenders did not give up. Indeed for some considerable time the battle was at an impasse, when finally Dinogad of Powys arrived, some six weeks after the fray had started, and swung the balance of power, giving the battle to Ryderych and his allies.

The outcome in Ryderych's favour changed the balance of military strength in the land of Pryden, the area between the two Roman walls. His victory enabled him in time to expand his territory into what became the British Kingdom of Strathclyde.

This defeat was, of course, a disaster for Aidan who, having rushed to support his wife's cousin Gwendalleau, had expected support not only from Cynfarch O'Oer but also from his two powerful sons Urien and Loth. This was not to be and even though Gwendelleau was not acceptable to them as a stepfather, it would seem that self-interest was a more obvious motive.

Now Aidan, fleeing from the defeat of Arftyrydd, sought the shelter of Urien of Rheged, his relative by marriage, whose Hall was at Caer Laverock, and who eventually saw him safely back to Dalriada.

It is thought that Aidan's experience of battle at Arftyrydd excited him to a love of battle, so that thereafter he never shunned a fight and, win or lose, he was involved in a great many of them from the Isle of Man to Orkney, though he is claimed to have disgraced his sword for having fled the field of Arftyrydd.

His meeting with Urien of Rheged at this time seems to have created a good relationship between them. After this, Aidan was always willing to help Rheged should the need arise.

This need arose on at least two occasions. When Urien attacked the Northumbrians and drove them from the mainland on to the Farne Islands, he was assisted by Scots mercenaries supplied, it is thought, by Aidan's kinsman, King Fiachna from Northern Ireland, Aidan being otherwise engaged with battles of his own.

The other occasion was after Urien's son Owain's death, when he went to the aid of Rheged and met the Inglis at Degsastan in AD 603 (Dega's stone, probably Dalstane or Dawstane Rig in Liddlesdale). Although inflicting many casualties, he lost the day. From then on the Inglis controlled much of the land between the two Walls.

It is possible that Aidan's son Artur was sent to Rheged, to be fostered and have his education as a warrior completed at Urien's hands at Caer Laverock, and he may well have been accompanied by his sister Gwyar, who later married Urien's brother Low or Loth.

Professor N.L. Goodrich, in support of the findings of R.L. Graeme Ritchie, believes that Artur may have been born at Caer Laverock, and that his mother occupied the fortress. However, the explanation offered here is of Artur spending time at Caer Laverock, to finish off his education, and there meeting and marrying the daughter of Gwrtheyrn Gwrtheneu, son of Gwydol, son of Dyfnwal Hen, descendants of Coel Hen Godebog. This meant that his mother-in-law occupied Caer Laverock with her husband, who was an advisor to Urien, and from his name, a Chief of the Cornovii in his own right, through the distaff side of his family.

Their daughter's name was Gwenwhyvawr. This seems a more likely and acceptable explanation.

Interestingly enough, Gwrtheyrn Gwrtheneu had another daughter, called Madrun, who became Eliffer Gosgordfawr's second wife, and mother to Peredur and Gwrgi.

CHAPTER 8
NENNIUS, 9TH CENTURY SCRIBE

*Then the warrior Arthur, with the soldiers and
Kings of Britain, used to fight against them. And
though there were many of more noble birth than
he, he was twelve times leader in war and victor
of the battles.*

Nennius, *Historia Brittonum*

As discussed in the introduction, Nennius, working in Bangor, north
Wales, in the very early part of the ninth century, had access to a mish-
mash of notes, family histories and genealogies, as well as verbal
traditions in bardic poem and song. It is possible he may have set
down some of the verbal traditions himself, which he compiled into a
history of some sorts, his *Historia Brittonum*. He did not edit or
catalogue his information, but let it come out as a series of seemingly
non-related incidents.

This work along with others is contained in the Harleian Manuscript
No. 3859, which is a miscellany of historical and fabled stories,
probably from early documents set down by a Scriptorum in St David's
monastery in the very south-west corner of Wales (see Professor Leslie
Alcock's book *Arthur's Britain*). Somehow Nennius got access to it,
enabling him to adapt it into his sort of history.

It must be stressed that Nennius's genealogia and family histories

73

are principally of the Northern Britons the *Gwyr Y Gogledd*, i.e., families north of a line roughly drawn from the mouth of the River Humber to the middle of Cardigan Bay, round about the town of Aberdyfi at the mouth of the River Dovey.

His genealogia (Folio 195A–195B) forms the basis of the present day Ancient Welsh Genealogies. Later scribes added to and brought up to their date his basic work. *We place a high regard on these family trees, and use them to support our case, wherever possible*, particularly those entries that can be ascribed and located before the middle of the eighth century, solely derived from Bardic recitation and training.

Nennius had knowledge of an epic poem or song, praising a minor hero in an age of Heroic Britons, a man of the north whose hall was soon to be overrun by the enemy, the Inglis or Northumbrians, who divided Britons of the north from their cousins in the south by the battle of Chester, *c.* AD 615/616. Hence his praises were not long sung in his own hall, but were remembered occasionally by the bards and minstrels of the southern Britons. In the early ninth century Nennius rediscovered this man called Arthur, which is a Saxon name for the Celtic one of Artir, Artur or Arddur or a number of other possible spellings.

Britain at this time, including its Saxon or Teutonic settlers, was undergoing a threat of invasion from the Vikings, and was therefore in great need of some sort of a Hero, to reinvigorate the people. Indeed, it forced the imperious Saxons of the south to unite under a Northumbrian King, Ecgberht II: something of a comedown for them, especially since their Great King Alfred had just united the various Saxon tribes into one Saxon nation and given future England its basic laws. Nonetheless, it was this amalgamation of the Saxons with the Inglis or Northumbrians to form in the ninth century the Anglo Saxon Nation, that just defeated the Norsemen in their attempt at the subjugation of our island. Certainly the Britons on their own could never have done it.

This was the background to Nennius's reintroduction of a person called Arthur, who became a super-hero, a man who would come back from the dead and save Britain!

Now Nennius merely reported what he knew, but later so-called historians, for example Geoffrey of Monmouth, took his work and, not being good speakers of the old British tongue, guessed at most of his translations and in addition fabulised Nennius's straightforward interpretations. Later still, mediaeval reporters or storytellers embellished them with mediaeval chivalry, with princes, knights, tournaments and court magicians and so on, things unheard of in sixth century Britain.

The Britons' idea of Kingship was very hazy – they recognised Chiefs, or High Chiefs; our word for King had not been adopted yet from the Saxon word *cyng*, and Princes and Princesses had not been invented!

It is little wonder that later historians could not identify Arthur, with all the misinformation that was being attributed to him. In fact, so much fame was being attached to him that it would have been completely impossible for history to lose him. It is by realising that he was a minor Brythonic Hero, in a less well-known part of the country, less well-known that is, as far as the main writers of our early history were concerned, the southern scribes being ignorant of things or happenings north of Hadrian's Wall, that it becomes sensible to lose such a person. Only in this context does it come within the bounds of reasoned argument or understanding.

It is worse, when acceptable history confirms a person of this actual name, at the correct time, then excludes him from consideration on the grounds of his nationality, i.e., as the son of an Iro-Scot, little realising, it seems, that his grandmother was British, his mother was British, and that he married a British woman and so was of the Britons. This is especially significant as British tribes were matrilineal, passing title and land rights through the women, who were very powerful and did not always give up their right to lead the tribe to their husband. Some insisted on being Chieftainesses themselves, e.g. Boudicca and Cartimandua, while Essylly, daughter of Cynan, last King of the line of Maelgwyn Gwynedd, gave Gwynedd on marriage to Mervyn Frych, Chief in Mannau Gododdin in the north, leading to the Great Rhodri Mawr, their son, being the over King of all, or most of, Wales.

This has been our different approach, looking at the relationships of these powerful women with the men they married and how it affected their actions in history. We feel it has given a much more balanced and explanatory historic view than we have had up to present.

Nennius names a successful war leader of the Britons (note, not a King), then describes a number of successful battles fought by this leader, Artur, twelve in all, which brought a number of years of peace to his region. This spell of some eight years of peace made Artur and his followers unwary and less sensitive to undercurrents, particularly in observing the developing relationship between Arthur's nephew Modred and his wife Gweny.

We have explained how Artur was in charge of his mother's estates in the east. He was the local laird, or petty 'King', and decided to go on a visit to his father Aidan in Dalriada, leaving his wife in charge of his estates, little realising of the love affair between Gweny and Modred.

Modred, now Chief in Fife or Fortren, with the connivance of Gwenwhyvawr, moved to take advantage of the situation of Artur's absence to usurp his protectorate, well knowing that there would be retribution, but that they would have the advantage of time in their preparation for the inevitable resulting battle, in other words, the choice of site would be theirs. To be sure of enough troops, Modred involved the Maetae of Clackmannan, who either owed him a favour or were subject to his Chieftaincy of the Venicones.

In this they were proved correct. They selected a position in Strath Carron, suitable for their purpose, and awaited the coming onslaught.

Word of the treachery reached Dalriada. Aidan prepared to defend his wife's inheritance, and retaliate for the insult to his son Artur. Never one to shun an opportunity for a fight, he made hurried preparations and set off to redress the situation, with his eldest sons Eochid Find and Artur. If we have any criticism of Aidan's actions in his lifetime, it is that he did not make the best preparations for battle but rushed them, and tended to underestimate his enemy.

This is the battle we have described earlier, St Columba's, Miathi, our Maetae *c.* AD 582, in Saxon, *Camlan*, in Cumbric, *Camelon* or *Carron*, where Eochid Find and Artur were killed. W.F. Skene's *Kir Kin* = Cair Rin or Carron. Dr Bannerman, however, in his work *Studies in the History of Dalriada*, identifies Kir Kin as a later battle at the Pictish capital of Fortren, around AD 596 (Annal of Ulster), in which Aidan's sons Bran and Domangart are killed, and considers that it is a different battle from Columba's Miathi, and we wholly agree with Dr Bannerman's assessment.

St Columba had a vision of the Miathi battle and declared Aidan had been victorious, but was sorry for him, because he had lost his eldest sons Eochaid Find and Artur.

This was a complete disaster. Modred was victorious and took Gweny to be 'Queen' in his lands in Fife, where verbal tradition has it she is buried in Meigle churchyard, Perthshire.

Aidan had to return a year later to fight the battle of Slamannan (Mannan *c.* 583), which Modred lost, and where Aidan regained his wife's estates and avenged his sons' deaths. Aidan was involved in three battles of Mannan or Mannand: one in *c.* 582, which we equate with Columba's Miathi; this one in *c.* 583 where he recovers his lost estates; and lastly a battle of Mannan or Euboniam, the Isle of Man, in *c.* 584, when Aidan defeated Baetean mac Cairill, King of the Dal Fiatach who had ruled in that island.

All these attempts by Aidan to protect his wife's birthright and support his wife's relations through marriage show him to be a man of his word, and not to be confused with the Briton, Aeddan Vraddog (the untrustworthy), son of Caw, killed at the battle of Catreath.

We have come full cycle from Nennius to the death of Artur, a fitting end to this chapter.

CHAPTER 9

ARTUR (ARTHUR)

Tho' Merlin sware that I should come again
To rule once more – but let what will be, be,
I am so deeply smitten thro' the helm
That without help I cannot last till morn.

Tennyson

We now introduce our candidate, Artur, attested for in the late seventh century by St Adamnan, biographer of the life of St Columba, who was the first Abbot of Iona, long before a mention of a person of this name by Nennius in the ninth century.

St Adamnan tells us that in one of St Columba's discourses with Aidan, he asks Aidan which of his eldest sons does he think will succeed him? Aidan replies: either his eldest son Eochaid Find, or his second son Artur. Saint Columba says, 'No', and tells him to send for his younger children, and that when they enter, the one who climbs on to his knee and hugs him will be the one to succeed him. This was Eocho' Bui.

Another time St Adamnan states that when Aidan and his two eldest sons are engaged in the battle of the Miathi (the Maetae tribe), St Columba in a vision claims Aidan to be victorious, but sad that he has lost his two eldest sons Eochaid Find and Artur in the battle.

In this prediction St Columba was not correct. It was a defeat, but

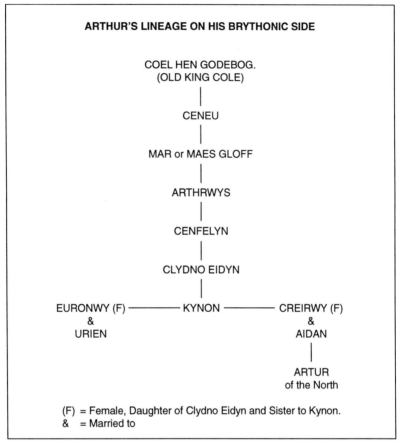

Table 1

as with Myrddin (Merlin) a lot of his predictions were more wishful thinking and did not always prove true. These are probably the earliest mentions of a historical character called Artur in Britain.

Despite these confirmations by St Adamnan of an Artur, a son of Aidan of Dalriada in the sixth century, he is generally disregarded by later historians as a possible candidate for the historic person of Artur of the romantic tales, because he is the son of an Iro-Scot, hence not a Briton or of the Britons.

This is a completely erroneous view. His grandmother is Lluan, a Briton from south Wales, so his father is half British. His father marries a British woman (we suggest Creirwy, daughter of Clydno Eidyn, sister to Euronwy wife of Urien of Rheged) and so Artur is three-quarters British. Lastly, Artur himself marries a British woman, Gwenwhyvawr, daughter of Gwrtheyrn Gwrtheneu.

This line of descent from Gabhran has, through the female side, reverted back to its British heritage rather than to its Iro-Scottish origins. This is celebrated through bardic verse and song, contained in many of the works of the four ancient Bards and Books of Wales.

The line did not return to its Scottish parts until the Britons of Strathclyde joined in with the newish Scottish Kingdom (founded in the ninth century by Kenneth Mac Alpine) early in the eleventh century, and so lost the British way of saying 'son of', i.e., 'Ap' or 'Map', and replaced it with the Scottish 'Mac' or 'Mc'.

Artur's father Aidan, half British himself, married into a powerful Britonic family practising matrilineal succession, and gained the Lairdship of his wife's estates of Camelon and Avolond, through on the River Forth, which involved him in a number of seemingly irrational decisions in his early life. These can only be explained by the influence of his wife. For instance, he, a Christian, soon to be ordained King by St Columba, joins a battle against a Christian alliance, on the side of non-Christians, because the non-Christian Chief is his wife's cousin.

By the time the battle of Arftyrydd looms on the horizon, Artur would be in his late teens, say eighteen or nineteen years old. When the battle actually threatens, Aidan, although a Christian, supports his wife's cousin Gwendalleau, a non-Christian, leaving his wife's estates in the care of his elder sons, and goes to war. The outcome has already been discussed: Aidan has to flee to Dalriada, where he is made sixth King.

This altered his relationship with his Brythonic family. He could no longer give his time to his wife's lands, and now he wanted his eldest son Eochaid Find, whom he expected to succeed him, and his wife Creirwy, through in Dalriada at his side, leaving his second son Artur in control of his wife's inheritance. This was the Lairdship of Camelon and Avolond and the responsibility required also the defence of the eastern end of the Antonine Wall from northern marauders and sea raiders on the upper reaches of the River Forth.

This was Artur's task, in an alliance with his brother-in-law Low or Loth of Lothian, to guard the south shore of the Firth of Forth, while his nephew Modred, now Chief in Fife, guarded the northern shore. This would appear to be an ideal alliance, both from a family and from a military point of view. However the relationship between Artur and his nephew Modred left much to be desired, and is given special scrutiny later.

Just as Nennius stated, Artur was not a King, but a war leader who turned out to be the son of a King. Because of where he found himself located by circumstances, he was in the right place at the right time when the Inglis or Northumbrians, led by Eocha, the son of Hengist, King of the Kent Jutes, and Ebissa (his nephew) with their descendants, who had settled on the upper reaches of the River Forth, began to expand aggressively towards the west, with the support of Pictish allies.

Hengist's father Vecta, who must have accompanied Eocha, confirming that some Jutish Saxons had reached the far north in collusion with the Inglis, is said to be buried at the Cat Stane, situated on the south bank of the River Almond, where the River Almond forms a boundary for Edinburgh Airport, right next to Ingliston (Inglis Town) so named to this day. It is claimed that a Latin inscription on the stone to that effect was discernible in the seventeenth century. 'Cat' or 'Cath' meant 'a battle', thus Cat Stane, a stone marking the place of a battle.

Artur was in charge of his mother's estates of Camelon and Avolond and was defender of the eastern end of the Antonine Wall. Hence he had to act swiftly and took on the role of War leader, fighting, according to Nennius, twelve successful battles against the Inglis who were probably in alliance with the Northern Picts or Caledones. These fights were in and around the Forth-Clyde Valley and the Woods of Caledon. His victory brought some eight or so years of peace to the area.

Plate 2: Cat Stane, near Edinburgh,
viewed by James Drummond in 1849

The Fables claim a peace lasting anywhere from ten to some twenty or so years, which we dispute, as the warrior clans relied on the 'Fighting Season' to build their reputation for bravery and ferocity in battle, and would soon depart from the hall of a lord who did not offer an opportunity to increase their reputations. Even the eight years of peace claimed in this rendering would require a leader of extraordinary personality to keep his war bands or *Gosgordfawrs* together and at peace for such a time. In fact, shortly after Artur's death, Urien of Rheged, Artur's mentor, seems to have gone on a cattle raid into what were Artur's lands in Mannau Gododdin! (See Taliesin's poem '*Bei Lleas Urien*' (What if Urien were Dead), translation by Meirion Pennar.)

It is felt that his main claim to fame is that he fought these twelve battles in one short fighting season, which was spring and summer, a considerable feat not only of arms but of logistics. There is nothing in the saga that Nennius rediscovered that suggested Artur's battles were fought over a number of years or fighting seasons.

This suggests that the majority of the battles were, in fact, skirmishes and chases, exaggerated by the British bards to show up the prowess of their hero in battle.

The order that the battles were fought needs a little modification after the identifications of W.F. Skene and S. Glennie. The battles had resulted from an attack on the Britons of Cadzow (the battle of Goddeu), who were farmers and not used to fighting, by the Inglis aided by a small number of Kentish Jutes, as they are described as non-Christian, and their allies, probably apostate Picts or Caledones.

These farmers of Cadzow were led by one Gwyddion, and hid themselves in Cadzow Wood, camouflaged as trees, conducting a guerilla warfare to defeat their attackers. This brought Artur into the field supported by, it would seem, his nephew Gwalchmai with a *Gosgordfawr* of troops (300 men) from Mynyd Agned (Dun Eidin, Edinburgh).

Cadzow was in Ryderych's lands (present day Hamilton in Lanarkshire) where he, as defender of the western end of the Wall, was not amused. His relations with his adversary Aidan's son Artur would be strained, to say the least, and it is suspected that his complaint about the poor defence of the eastern end of the Wall, allowing intruders to spread so far west without opposition, spurred Artur to immediate action, without recourse to advice from his father Aidan who was probably at the convention of Drumcett.

The Northumbrians, after their defeat by the Britons of Cadzow, moved south, deep into the Caledon wood, to regroup and await events now that their aggressive intentions were known. There was bound to be a backlash.

That backlash was Artur with his men, who located and made contact with the Llogres (English) at the River or Water of Glen where it joins the River Irvine at Darvel in the parish of Loudon, Ayrshire.

There was a skirmish and the Inglis withdrew westwards to the Water of Bath near the small town of Beith, Ayrshire (the battle of Beit as reported on by the Bard Taliesin). Again the Inglis withdrew northward to the River Clyde which they crossed, landing at the mouth of the River Leven (Argoed Llwyfein perhaps), where they prepared to make a stand against Artur's waterborne chase.

They were again forced to withdraw to the south banks of Loch Lomond, in Lennox (Linneas), where a number of battles were fought in and around the Glen of Dubglas (Douglas) and the upper and lower rivers of that name. All were overlooked by the mountain Ben Arthur, and always Artur was victorious.

The invaders were then forced along the line of the Antonine Wall, eastwards towards their port of entry on the Forth, and along the Strath of Carron to Dunipaice where, on the River Bonny, the next skirmish took place.

The Northumbrian general Ossa Cyllellaur, son of Ebissa, then hit upon a daring plan. His intelligence made him aware that among his pursuers were men from Dun Eidin, leaving that city under-defended. He decided to strike a blow upon the Britons by capturing Dinas Eidin, Edinburgh, sweeping through it and on to the top of what is now Artur's Seat. This gave them a view of the River Forth, so that when their ships arrived at the Water of Leith, they could make a concerted charge down Mont Agned to the Leith shore for a quick embarkation, and then sail south to their stronghold of Bambro' Castle and safety.

Artur, hot on their heels, did not give them time to settle, but chased them off Mont Agned which became Arthur's Seat, forcing them to the south through the Wood of Cleyddon, fighting a battle on the way. He followed them to the valley of the Gala Water (old name Wedale) and defeated the Saxons of the east coast, which suggests that the Inglis might have been reinforced from the east or south. Artur turned the Inglis northwards, forcing them into his own lands of Avolond in the plain of Slamannan. There they made a last stand on the Iron Age fort on the top of the hill of Bowden (Bawdon), just a few miles south-east of Artur's Hall of Camelon. The Inglis left a small rearguard on the ford known as the 'Fechtin' Ford', which did not hold Artur up. Here at Bowden Hill, the Llogres were thoroughly and finally defeated.

The usual thing in those days, when a battle was to be fought close to the seat or hall of one of the protagonists, was for the non-combatants to sally out to a point of vantage to watch the outcome of the fight. This had advantages: if the battle was going their way, after the successful outcome they could praise the prowess of their leader and victorious troops; on the other hand, should the day go against them, they had the maximum warning to flee for safety.

This was the case here, and Gwenwhyvawr and Modred left Camelon and proceeded to the vantage point of the hill immediately opposite Bowden, next to Linlithgow town. Ostensibly they went to watch the outcome of the battle, but lust was in the air and either Gweny seduced Modred or Modred seduced Gwenwhyvawr. Whichever, the hill has been known ever since as Cockleroy Hill, the hill on which the local King was cuckolded! In other words, Artur was betrayed by his wife and nephew here.

It is then stated that during his fights or skirmishes, he took four great fortresses: Kaer Lium, Fort of Leven or Dumbarton; Stirling at Tratheu Tryweryd or Carse of Stirling; Mynyd Agned, Edinburgh defended by the Cath Bregion, or mixed peoples or Picts, their allies; and the last battle at the Hill of Bowden, an Iron Age fort in the centre of the country between these strongholds. This makes the number of battles or skirmishes fought subject to surmise.

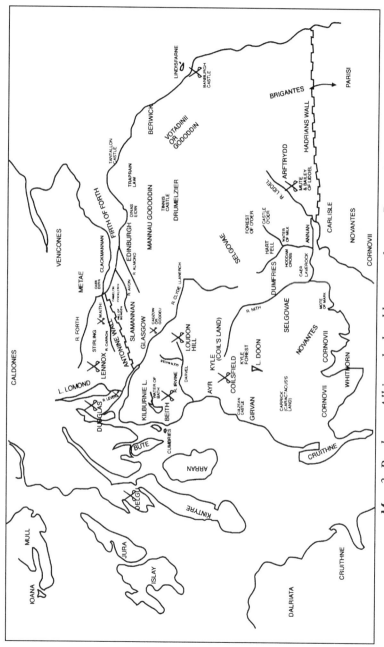

Map 3: Pryden or Albion, the land between the two Roman Walls

It is significant that when defeating the Inglis at the River Leven's mouth, this battle or skirmish must have been observed by Ryderych Hael from his fort of Alcluyd, on the summit of Dumbarton Rock. Yet he is not anywhere reported to have gone to Artur's aid, and perhaps this gives rise to the report that Artur *unaided by anyone* killed some nine hundred of the enemy, an exaggerated criticism of Ryderych and other Chiefs for not giving him any support, although Urien of Rheged seems to have aided him, according to Taliesin.

True there is some great play made in the tales about his famous sword, Caliburn or Excalibur, which suggests he was a swordsman extraordinary; however, sticking to what is believed to be more real history, it is his abilities as a War leader that got him an Epic poem or Saga, along with the other Men of the North, the *Gwyr Y Gogledd.*

Unfortunately not long after his death, following their success at the battle of Chester, the Northumbrians spread north into south-east Scotland, overrunning Mannau Gododdin and Camelon and Avolond, and Artur's Hall was no more.

However his poem or song of praise was occasionally recounted in the halls of his Brithonic cousins in the south in unconquered Wales. It was brought back into the light of day by Nennius in the ninth century.

Artur's sister, who was called Gwyar, was wife of Low or Loth of Lothian in the tribal lands of the Roman Gotadinii or British Gododdin tribe; by marrying Gwyar, Loth became Artur's brother-in-law.

Loth or Low was son of Cynfarch O'Oer, and he gained the Chieftaincy to the Gotadinii tribe by a first marriage to Bellicent, a Chieftainess or Queen of Orkney and the Gododdin. She predeceased him, and he allied himself with Dalriada by marrying Aidan's daughter Gwyar. He had at least two sons, Modred by his first wife, Queen of Orkney, and Gwalchmai by Artur's sister Gwyar, his second wife. This makes Modred a nephew of Artur by marriage only, whilst Artur is a blood relative of his other nephew, Gwalchmai.

Artur's relationship with each of these two nephews was entirely different. Modred's attitude to his uncle appeared to be very resentful, whilst Gwalchmai (Sir Gawain or Gawayne) was always full of loyalty and support. Artur and Modred could be of an age with each other.

In addition, when Artur took Gwenwhyvawr to wife, daughter of Gwrtheyrn Gwrtheneu (a Chief, in his own right, of the Cornovii and advisor to Urien), it is suspected she was already the object of Modred's desire; and so sealed his resentment of Artur.

This culminated in his seduction of her on Cockleroy Hill. Then he usurped Artur's lairdship, whilst Artur was away on a visit to his father in Dalriada. Thus he brought Artur to battle in Strath Carron, where he killed Artur and claimed Gweny as his prize, taking her to his lands in Fife and there making her his 'Queen'.

It is reported that when she died she was buried in the churchyard at Meigle, in the old district of Angus.

This battle in the tales is called Camlan, a derivation of Camelon, in truth the battle of Camlann Guotadin in the district of the Gotadini or Gododdin tribe in the north. The Dalriadans called it the battle of the Miathi (Maetae tribe) fought in Strath Carron, c. AD 582, at which Artur and his elder brother Eochaid Find were killed.

It is not known whether Artur and his brother were buried on the battlefield, or left as carrion or taken back to Dalriada by Aidan to be buried on Iona, with the blessing of St Columba. This last option is the most likely, but his grave and that of his brother are unknown, as stated in the *Black Book of Carmarthen*.

Aidan returned to avenge his sons' deaths and, in c. 583, fought the battle of Slamannan (Mannan) in which he was victorious, regaining his wife's inheritance.

To the Dalriadans there was nothing extraordinary about Artur and his battles – they were used to battles almost every day – and Aidan as an example to his children was continually on the move fighting some battle or another.

Artur's mother Creirwy was a daughter of Clydno Eidyn, and sister to Kynon, the only sure person to escape from the battle of Catreath, as depicted in the poem 'The Gododdin', by the Bard Aneirin. Kynon was Artur's uncle, and Gwendalleau was Kynon's uncle, killed at Arftyrydd. She was sister to Euronwy, wife to Urien of Rheged. This shows his relationship to the most important and powerful families of the British, to be sung by the *Cerddor* (minstrels), told by the *Cyfarwydd* (story tellers) and eulogised by the *Bardds* or *Prydydd* (poets).

W.F. Skene, that illustrious Victorian historian, took the Arthurian fables by the shoulders and shook them, to reveal, hidden away in early British bardic poetry and song, details of the history of the Ancient Britons. He brought into the sunlight of understandable history a real person, Artur, a sixth century hero of the *Cymry* or *Combrogi* and the *Gwyr Y Gogledd*, a Man of the North.

Unfortunately, Skene, too, did not consider Artur son of Aidan, as he was not apparently of the Britons, whereas not only was he more than half British, but he spent his life leading and fighting for the Britons. Artur married a woman of the Britons, making his children more British than Scottish! Hence he is adopted into the role of British Hero, and rewarded by the Brythonic Bards recounting his exploits.

W.F. Skene and a number of others have confused Aidan son of Gabhran, whose family tree they take back to Macsen Weldig, with a British Aeddan Vradog. Aidan son of Gabhran is however really Iro-Scots leading back to Ercc of the Ui Neil in Dalriata, Northern Ireland, whilst this Aeddan Vradog who fought in the north and was killed at the battle of Catreath appears to be the son of Caw of Pryden.

When present day Scots sing of Caledonia, they are singing the praises of the ancient Britons of these northern lands, not of the later conquering Dalriadia Scots.

Attached to Artur is the legend of his prowess as a swordsman, whether due to his prowess or to the magical properties of his weapon, we shall not investigate.

His sword's name in Brythonic is Caladfwlch or Caledvwlch (Shining Blade), but in Saxon is Caliburn, 'the sword forged on the burn of the Caledonians'. This is very near the truth, the real meaning being 'the sword forged on the Carron Burn', most certainly in the land of the Caledonians.

The earliest iron ore deposits in Scotland (Albion) were to be found on the banks of the River Carron a few miles from Camelon. Indeed, iron and coal continued to be worked there from the earliest times right through to the twentieth century, when the Carron Iron Works ceased production of iron castings in the late 1960s.

As usual the southern scribes, with their very limited knowledge of the northern British people or the geography of early Britain north of the Hadrian Wall, knew that the sword was forged on a burn of the Caledons, hence its name, Caliburn – but did not know the burn's name. When we come to look at Sir Thomas Malory and his *Le Morte D'Arthur*, the sword is called Excalibur, which means 'from Caliburn' (*ex* is Latin prefix = from + Calibur(n)). Both mean the same, the sword from the Caledon's burn, which is the only magical thing about this sword, and one must come to the conclusion that it was Artur's ability as a swordsman that it is the historic truth. Artur, as the local Laird, would have his sword made locally by his iron masters on his estate on the Carron burn in Camelon, i.e. Caliburn! It was no doubt claimed to have enchanted skills by the smith, working with his knowledge of weight, balance and temper.

When swords were the principal weapons of the times, they understandably became the object of extraordinary powers. Sir Walter Scott in his 'Lady of the Lake', in notes to Canto 2, writes, 'The ancient warriors whose hope and confidence rested chiefly in their blades, were accustomed to deduce omens from them, especially from such as were supposed to have been fabricated by enchanted skills, of which we have various instances in the Romances and Legends of the times.'

The wonderful sword Skofnung wielded by the celebrated Hrolf Kraka was of this description. It was deposited in the tomb of the Monark on his death, and taken from thence by Skeggo, a celebrated pirate who bestowed it upon his son-in-law Kormak with the following instructions:

"The manner of using it will appear strange to you. A small bag is attached to it, which take heed not to violate. Let not the rays of the sun touch the upper parts of the handle, nor underneath it, unless thou art ready for battle, but when thou comest to the place of fight go aside from the rest, grasp and extend the sword, and breathe upon it, then a small worm will creep out of the handle: lower the handle that he more easily may return to it."

'Kormak, having received the sword, returned home to his mother. He showed her the sword and attempted to draw it though unnecessary, and ineffectually for he could not pluck it out of the sheath. His mother Dalla exclaimed, "Do not despise the counsel given to thee, my son." Kormak, however, repeating his efforts, pressed down the handle with his feet and tore off the bag, when Skofnung emitted a hollow groan, but still he could not unsheath the sword. Kormak then went out with Bessus, whom he had challenged to fight with him, and drew apart at the place of combat. He sat down upon the ground, ungirdling his sword which he bore above his vestments. He did not remember to shield the hilt from the rays of the sun. In vain he endeavoured to draw it, till he placed his foot against the hilt, then the worm issued from it. But Kormak did not rightly handle the weapon in consequence whereof good fortune deserted it.'

From this rather long story of Skofnung it is not difficult to imagine the magical powers imputed to Caliburn or Excalibur when wielded by Artur, and his skill as a swordsman when wielding his locally made sword, presumably under his own supervision on his own forge in his own lands.

Further evidence to support the Caliburn's origin in north Britain would seem to be Arthur's O'Oen, Arthur's oven or forge, just north of Camelon in Falkirk. This Romanesque building, built with unmortared stone, is attributed to the second century. It was in the shape of what now would be called a mausoleum, and purported to be the repository for the Standards of the Legions who built and manned the Antonine Wall. Its purpose is not really known. It might have housed a small sports arena, for the Roman soldiers manning the fort of Camelon to use for their recreation.

However, on the Romans' withdrawal it deteriorated, the dome probably collapsing, and was put back into military use by the Mannawins who turned it into a forge, its open dome being ideal for this purpose, for producing weapons from their rich iron ore deposits. Artur's sojourn as his mother's laird in Camelon brought about his association with the forge, and hence the name Arthur's O'Oen (oven). It was unfortunately demolished in the seventeenth century, leaving only drawings of the building to show us what it looked like, although at Sir John Clerk's estate at Penicuik, Midlothian, there is a replica of it built as a dovecot.

Another essential piece of Arthurian equipment is the Round Table of which much is made. It was introduced into the tales by Wace, an Anglo-Norman of the twelfth century, and later expanded by Malory and others.

There are many ways to describe the uses to which the Round Table could be used. To sit in a circle is a quite natural thing to do: one always sits round a camp fire. It allows all those of the tribe or association or friends to see each other and hear each other's discourses to advantage. In open air gatherings it permits look-outs to see in all directions, more than ever of course in respect of military affairs.

It is in this sense and in the time of Arthurian battles which were often mere skirmishes, that the leader at appropriate times would require foot soldiers to erect turfwall surrounds, serving as tables, to discuss military tactics and manoeuvres and at the same time used as tables upon which food would be placed. This is what Agricola did in his northern campaigns, staying each night behind turf walls and wooden palisades.

Somehow, when people look back in time towards a particular happening or notable person, it is mostly the romantic recollections which prevail rather than the historic. This is particularly true of the Dark Ages when there were few historians available to record the times. Even then it was mostly monks who did these works, and of course their writings were biased by the influence of religion.

The subject of immediate interest is the Arthurian Round Table. Surely it is one of the most difficult of the legends to understand, yet it may be one of the most easily explained. Here we have a Britain in turmoil, and the struggle for power well advanced. Skene identifies Artur in twelve battles (Geoffrey of Monmouth also gives him twelve, both following Nennius) and it appears that throughout this time the legend of the Round Table gained in credence. Was it true? Professor Goodrich asks what was it and where was it?

One claim was that 250 sat at it during the August session of Artur's Court. Another was that the 'Queen' brought a hundred knights, still another that there were ninety knights brought to Artur's Court, while Geoffrey of Monmouth claimed that Artur had a Cornish carpenter who made a round table to seat 1,600 Knights at a meal. Chrétien de Troyes lost count after ten, then added another two or three or more.

On the face of it they cannot all be right, if the ordinary view of a table is considered. One which seated 1,600 would have a circumference of say 3,200 feet, while that of one hundred would require only 200 feet. Yet there is a possibility that both may have been true! *Where was it?* We can accept that Artur spent much of his effort, manoeuvring for some twelve or so battles, across the land bounded by the Antonine and Hadrian Walls with an army of considerable, though no doubt of a variable, size. From time to time they fought to preserve their land from the ever dangerous advance of the Angles or Inglis with some Jute and Saxon help.

From this it is clear that this would be an army on the move. It is also clear that such a force, whatever the size, must stop from time to time in order to rest, dress wounds, repair arms and perhaps bury their dead. Such places, not being permanent, would easily be formed into a rough turf mound around the leader, where he, occupying a central position at his own 'table' with his subordinates, would lecture the common soldiery while they ate or carried out other duties.

The size of these places would in some cases differ according to the number of troops required for each encounter. Resting places, guard areas as well as retreats, could well use old and more permanent locations, some of which may help explain a lot of the curious earthworks still visible today. For example, Artur's Knott at Stirling Castle is a candidate for the Round Table. William of Worcester in the fifteenth century stated that King Arthur presided over the Round Table at Stirling known as Snowdon West Castle.

It is now possible to think in terms of a large area in use by the common soldiery and a small central space in wood or stone, the whole acquiring the name of 'Arthur's Table'. This small central item would be transported with the army, though it is doubtful if the small table alone could work in such a way as to fire the imagination of poets and others, as it has done through the years.

Alternatively when a conference was called at a permanent base, each member would provide his own chair and individual table, which when placed in a circle would form a table of any size. Whatever the name of this formation, it was never intended to be taken literally. The important part is the creation of the circle as a means of democratic equality for the members. Generally, it would not be as democratic as all that, as the elder members would tend to sit next to the Chief, forcing new members to be located at the bottom opposite and away from the leader. In some courts the King sat on a dais, apart from the round table, in others in the centre.

In the Arthurian fables, the Round Table is used to show how democratic Artur is, and it is assumed that the Chief did not have a special seat or particular place on the circle, so that all who sat down were equal. The name is not important but the idea is!

It is thought necessary to raise this matter and discuss it in some detail, for the satisfaction of those who find it difficult to accept much of the Artur story unless there is a congruence to most of the legends. This would appear so in the case of Caliburn and the Round Table.

In the mediaeval tales, despite much fabulisation and change, there were a number of early British names that can be recognised as belonging to the fifth or sixth centuries as associates of Artur. They are:

Guinevere who is Gwenwhyvawr, daughter of Gwrtheyrn Gwrtheneu, son of Gwydol, descended from Coel Hen.

Merlin who is Myrddin, son of Morken, Chief of the Alcluyd Britons. Sage of the Selgovae. Nephew of Cynfarch O'Oer, and Ryderych Hael.

Modred or Medraut, son of Low or Llew of Lothian.

Gawain or (Sir) Gawayne, who is Gwalchmai, son of Low or Llew of Lothian.

Bedivere (Sir) who is Bedwyr or Brwydr Ddiriad (mischievous or unlucky), son of Gwyddien Astrus, son of Deigr, son of Dyfnwal Hen, descended from Coel Hen.

Kay who is Kei or Cei, associated with Dinas Eidin, Edinburgh.

Urien who is chief in Rheged, son of Cynfarch O'Oer of the Selgovae.

Ywain (Sir Ywain) who is Owain son of Urien of Rheged.

Percival (Sir) who is Peredur, possibly son of Eliffer Gosgordfawr, as there are a number of Peredurs.

Loth (Low or Llew) of Lothian, son of Cynfarch O'Oer.

All these ancient names, with the exception of Kay and Bedwyr or Brwydr, have been used in our story, and all tied up with our Artur.

Brwydr is in the genealogical tree of Coel Hen, although we have not directly associated him with Artur. Kay, or Cei, cannot be identified, although the surname McKay (pronounced Mac K-eye), could denote in southern Scotland (Albion), descendants of Kay.

Looking at what we know of this historical character: Artur, son of Aidan; the Arthur propounded by Geoffrey of Monmouth, based on a poem or song resuscitated by Nennius into an Arthur who virtually captures the sixth century known world.

If we start in the north with Iceland, then go south to the Baltic countries, we find that none of these countries have any reference to any capture by an Artur in their histories. He captures Saxony (Germany), Gaul (France), he is about to capture Italy and the Holy Roman Empire, when he has to abandon his actions and return to Britain, to deal with an insurrection by his nephew Modred. Despite this, none of the histories of these countries records any of this. It just does not make sense that such an all-conquering Hero's exploits in so many countries should now be lost to the histories of these countries. Worse, even lost to history in his own land.

Sense can only be made of the scrap of true history contained in Nennius's bardic verse: that of a local hero in a part of the country, the north, little known to the later southern scribes, and so lost to Saxon history.

But as Skene showed, contained in Britonic Bardic literature was history of the ancient Britons, and it is there that we find Artur, with his father.

We present Artur son of Aidan, son of Gabhran, as the historic model for Arthur of the mediaeval tales.

CHAPTER 10
MYRDDIN, BARD OF THE SELGOVAE

Sweet apple-tree
with flowers foxglove pink
that grows in secret
in the forest of Celyddon,
and even though
you look for it
it is all in vain

Myrddin: *Black book of Carmarthen*

At the battle of Arftyrydd, supporting his Chief Gwendalleau was Myrddin, Chief Druid, Bard and advisor to the Selgovae tribe. He read the portents and pronounced them good, so Gwendalleau engaged in the battle.

To Myrddin's great horror and despair, his Chief, his father Morken and possibly his sister's son were all killed, and the battle was eventually lost. He fled to Hart Fell in the forest and lands of Castle O'Oer, so getting some protection from his kinsman Cynfarch O'Oer.

Deranged, he became a 'Wild man of the Woods', cutting himself off from the society of his fellows. But the *Vita Merlini* tells us that his twin sister Gwenddydd, in trying to tempt him back to civilisation and sanity, built him a small stone temple; and there on Little Hart Fell just below Hart Fell is a small stone circle, still standing to this day.

If there is any truth in the poem, and if his sister really did build it for him, then it must be one of the last examples of a stone circle to be built in Britain – Myrddin's temple.

Myrddin eventually recovered himself to a degree, and started to leave his forest retreat, following the course of the Water of Milk down from Hart Fell to its junction with the River Annan. At Hoddam Mill and a little further along the Annan, at Hoddam Cross, he met with another kinsman, St Kentigern.

Fordun, the earliest Scottish historian, in *Chronicles of the Scottish Nation* tells the story of 'Kentigern and Llailoken'; the Brito-Pictish historical romance 'Llallogan', the *'Historia Beati Kentigerni'* and Jocellyn's 'Life of St Kentigern' all confirm that St Kentigern and Myrddin (Llailoken) met several times at Hoddam Cross where Kentigern was priest, and engaged in religious exchanges.

Myrddin is closely related to Cynfarch O'Oer. It is believed that his father Morken (or Mourig, his Selgovae name) was a brother to Cynfarch, a son of Meirchion Gul. Cynfarch was Myrddin's uncle, and he was cousin to Urien and Low or Loth, second cousin to Owain, Modred and Gwalchmai, and a cousin twice removed to St Kentigern.

One must remember that it was a prime duty of a Druid Priest and Bard to be the keeper of the family genealogy, to recite it by rote, as a precursor to learning the Bardic profession. Hence he recognised St Kentigern as a blood relation. He was kinsman to Urien, kinsman to Owain, Urien's son, and kinsman to Cyndeyrn Garthwys, son of Owain, namely St Kentigern who became St Mungo of Glasgow.

More importantly, he was the son of Morken, Mourig or Meurig, Chief of the Alcluyd Britons, and so nephew to Ryderych Hael. After Ryderych deposed his uncle, Myrddin's father, there was a great enmity between them.

When Morken was usurped, it was to his son Myrddin that he appealed for help, and it was Myrddin who, using his position as Chief

Druid in Gwendalleau's Hall, pressurised his Chief Gwendalleau into giving his father succour and protection.

This was what the battle of Arftyrydd was all about: deep family hatreds, where a mother and a father go to war against each other, dividing the loyalty of their family. Myrddin and his twin sister felt they had to support their father, whose very life was threatened, from the wrath of their mother, their uncle and their cousin Ryderych.

After a number of safe journeys from Hart Fell to Hoddam Cross, Myrddin began to lose his fear of Ryderych's vengeance and started to travel further afield. It is here suggested that he decided to visit a locale of his youth, and went on a visit to Tinnis Castle, an important Iron Age fort of the Selgovae, where it is again suggested that he was brought up and educated by his father's kinsmen, as was the generally accepted practice for a Chief's son in those early days.

Unfortunately, in the years since Arftyrydd, Ryderych Hael, the victor, had rapidly been expanding the influence of Alcluyd into what became know as Strathclyde, and had absorbed under his influence much of the lands of the Selgovae. This included the land surrounding Drumelzier, above which village is situated Tinnis Castle in the area still known today as Merlindale, in Peeblesshire.

In fact, shortly after the battle of Arftyrydd, the Selgovae seemed to move to the east and become part of the Gotadinii or Gododdin, and disappeared as a separate tribe.

Myrddin, unaware of these political changes, marooned in this forest retreat, set out on what was to prove to be his last journey, one for him of eager nostalgia. On reaching Drumelzier, he was recognised by shepherds, whose landlord Melredus was a supporter of Ryderych, and they attacked and slew him. He is purported to be buried in or near to Drumelzier churchyard.

It is possible that these shepherds were of a similar age to Myrddin, and may have known him during his fostered years, thus accounting for their recognition of him.

So ended the life of the last High Priest of the old Druid religion. He was a real historic person, Prophet and Bard of the Men of the North. There is a local legend that Ryderych's wife was having an affair with Melredus, and that Myrddin, in an attempt to reconcile himself with Ryderych, appraised him of the situation, so bringing the wrath of Melredus upon him.

He was right in the end, in his seemingly excessive fear of Ryderych's vengeance. While hiding on Hart Fell in the forest of O'Oer, he was wary of all strangers, as assassins sent by Ryderych. He had therefore to hide frequently from hunters, poachers, swineherds and others. His favourite hiding place was in an apple tree, where no doubt he ate the apples and, if they were juicy, was hidden, fed, and had his thirst assuaged.

It is the lines in the poem 'The Apple Tree' (Afallennau), attributed to him, that give us the clue to his lineage:

I am hated by Gwasawc, the supporter of Ryderych,
I have killed her son, and her daughter.

There are only two people known to be close relatives of Myrddin: a twin sister, Gwenddydd, and his father, Morfyn. We have always suspected that Morfyn could be Morken. They are both derivations of Morgan, as probably is Mourig or Meurig, Morken's family name.

The naming of Gwasawc, a female in the poem, using the translation given by Professor A.O.H. Jarman in N. Tolstoy's book *The Quest for Merlin*, allowed the deduction, because of matrilineal succession, that Gwasawc was married to Morken. They are his father and mother, both lines descended from Coel Hen Godebog. That Gwenddydd is his sister, is confirmed by the tract '*Cyfoesi Myrddin a Gwenddydd ei Chaer*', which translates from the Welsh as 'Conversations of Myrddin with Gwynddydd his sister'.

Most translations give Gwasawc as a male and friend of Urien of Rheged, but Jarman's translation, making Gwasawc female, gives an explanation of the events that makes it difficult to refute, and suggests a female warrior, or Chieftainess, who had the friendship of Urien. This could explain why he took no action when Rhyderych's or her forces crossed his territory on their way to Arftyrydd.

Myrddin's genealogy is as follows: Gwasawc is the eldest child and daughter of Clynog, Cedig or Ceredig (named after Coroticus or Ceredig, a contemporary of Coel Hen), son of Dyfnwal Hen, son of Gorwynion, and descended from Coel Hen Godebog. She is sister to Tudwald Tutclyd and his brother Serwan, and aunt to Rhyderych Hael, son of Tudwald Tutclyd. She held the rights to the Chieftaincy by matrilineal succession which she passed on to her chosen husband, who was Morken, or Mourig, son of Meirchion Gul, son of Gwrwst Ledlwm, son of Ceneu, son of Coel Hen.

Morken was brother to Cynfarch O'Oer.

The marriage of Gwasawc and Morken was blessed with twins, a boy Myrddin and a girl Gwenddydd.

All however did not remain well!

The interpretation of lines of the poem 'The Apple Tree' in the *Black Book of Carmarthen* is as follows:

I am hated by my mother Gwasawc, supporter of my hated nephew Ryderych who has killed her husband my father. Once I was the most respected High Priest, so that the land of Britain was called '*Clas Merdin*', my enclosure, and was related to many of the Great Chiefs; now look at me, a fugitive hiding in woods, shunned by everyone. Life has nothing to offer me or my sister, we might as well be dead. I have killed her [Gwasawc's] son, me, and her daughter, my sister, figuratively speaking

Ah me, Gwenddydd loves me not
The chiefs of Ryderych hate me,
After Gwenddolen no prince honours me,
Although at Ard'eryd I wore the golden torques.

Morken had sent his son to his kinsmen in the territory of the Selgovae to be educated. Myrddin decided to become a Druid Priest, and on achieving that objective was appointed Chief Druid and adviser to the tribe.

There were three grades of learned men: first, the Bards who were singers and poets; second, the Druids who were philosophers and theologians; and third, the Seers, who were interpreters of omens and sacrifices. Chief Druids like Myrddin and Emrys of Carmarthen often incorporated all three activities.

It may be that Myrddin put some pressure on his father in Alcluyd to revert back to the old Druid ways. In any event, Morken, it is suggested, started to oust the newish Christian religion in Alcluyd and reintroduce the old Druid one, much to the dismay of his wife Gwasawc, her brother Tudwald Tutclyd and his son Ryderych.

Jocellyn's life of St Kentigern states that Morken, King of Alcluyd, threatened the life of St Kentigern, so that he fled Glasgow and sought shelter with St David, who had trained under the mission of Candida Cassa, and King Catwallader in north Wales. Later, when Ryderych had ousted Morken, he recalled Kentigern to Glasgow.

They formed an opposition to Morken and, led by Ryderych, decided to depose and kill him. Ryderych ousted him from Alcluyd, and he fled for sanctuary to his son and his tribe the Selgovae. This caused Myrddin and his sister, with whom he seems to have kept up a close relationship, to support their father against their mother and her family, leading to the battle of Arftyrydd. A battle that could be about Christianity versus Druidism after all!

Ryderych was not satisfied with Morken's escape from Alcluyd. He wanted blood; and prepared for the battle of Arftyrydd, *c.* AD 573. His victory here with the death of Morken and Gwendalleau seemed to satisfy him. He felt much stronger; neither Cynfarch O'Oer, Urien nor Loth moved a finger to stop him. Only Aidan of Dalriada was to remain a thorn in his flesh.

Indeed Aidan may well have promised Myrddin to return with an army against Ryderych, if the ancient poem 'Peiryan Vaban' has any truth to it. Here Myrddin foretells that Aidan, now King in Dalriada, will be his avenging angel, and will come with an army and slay Ryderych.

There is some evidence that Aidan tried, but the outcome was not decisive and Rhyderych lived to fight again. He got St Kentigern to invite St Columba to visit Glasgow, then a village, in an attempt to placate Aidan's enmity through the Saint's friendship.

Myrddin is one of the Bards in the four ancient books of Wales. One account of the most telling is where there is a discourse between Myrddin and Taliesin on the merits of the battle of Arftyrydd. Taliesin takes the part of the Ryderych alliance, while Myrddin bewails or *foretells* the loss of the battle:

Ymddiddan Myrddin a Thaliesin

Taliesin
The host of Maelgwn, it was fortunate that they came –
Slaughtering men of battle, penetrating the gory plain,
Even the action of Ardderyd, when there will be a crisis,
Continually for the hero they will prepare.

Myrddin
A host of flying darts, reeking will be the gory plain,
A host of warriors, vigorous and active will they be;
A host, when wounds will be given, a host, when flight will take place,
A host, when they will return to the combat.

Taliesin
The seven sons of Eliffer, seven heroes when put to the proof,
They will not avoid seven spears in their seven divisions.

Myrddin
Seven blazing fires, seven opposing armies,
The seventh Cynvelyn in every foremost place.

Taliesin
Seven thrusting spears, seven rivers-ful
Of the blood of chieftains will they fill.

Myrddin
Seven score generous ones have gone to the shades;
In the wood of Celyddon they came to their end.
Since I, Myrddin, am next after Taliesin,
Let my prediction become common.

The other Chief Bards were:

Taliesin, who was the most prolific of the ancient ones. He was the Chief Bard in Urien's Hall in Rheged. Most of what we know of Urien and his son Owain comes from his work.

His birth is somewhat fabulised, involved with mysticism, which suggests that the Taliesin attached to Urien's Hall is called after a much more ancient and God-like person of the Britons.

His works include the descriptions of many battles of the northern Britons, some of which, we suspect, are separate descriptions of Artur's battles, e.g.:

I saw a brow covered with rage on Urien,
When he furiously attacked his foes at the white stone
Of Galystem.

This is Stuart Glennie's eighth battle of Castle Guinnion, near the Gala Water, in old Wedale, where, just above St Mary's Church at Stow, was a huge chalk stone that got broken during the construction of the new (then) Edinburgh to Carlisle road, now the A7 – the white stone of Galystem.

One of Taliesin's poems tells of the battle of Goddeu or Cadzow, where non-Christians, with allies, attacked the farmers of Cadzow, who retaliated by taking to the wood of Cadzow and, camouflaging themselves among the trees, fought and won a guerilla skirmish. Since their adversaries were non-Christian, it is likely they were Inglis or Northumbrians, with Caledones or Picts as allies. This action brought Artur into the field, to fight his twelve or so battles.

Llyarch Hen, another of the ancient Bards, belonged to the Selgovae tribe related to the Cynfarch O'Oer clan. He was son of Elidir Lydanwyn who was brother to Cynfarch. He was a warrior who supported his Lord Urien in battle against the Northumbrians, and took up the Bardic profession. Through the good offices of his cousin Low or Loth of Lothian, he was made resident Bard in Loth's most southerly stronghold, Dinguaroy (the Joyeuse Garde of the French romances), later to become Bambro' Castle.

Unfortunately, this was the first fort of the British to be captured by the Northumbrians in the north (by Ida, son of Eobba, King of Bernicia).

Llywarch Hen must have put up a spirited resistance, as he is shown as one of the Heroic Men of the North, but he had eventually to flee. Surprisingly he did not go north to his mentor Loth, nor to the west to his most favoured and powerful cousin Urien. He made instead a long trek to the south-west, to Powys in fact, and his decision to do this is only explained when one discovers that the Chief in Powys was Cynddylan, one of his many sons. This would appear to be another example of a son of a noble family leaving his homeland and travelling many miles, in this case from the land of O'Oer to Powys, to find a woman with the rights to the Clan Chieftaincy which is passed to her husband on marriage in matrilineal succession.

Llyarch Hen continued his profession of Bard in Powys, under his son's protection. Of his authorship is the poem 'Geraint, son of Erbin', in which Artur and Kai are linked with Dinas Eidin (Edinburgh).

He lived to an extremely old age, from Arthur's time to seventh century Cadwallon, suggesting an age of some 150 years. However, if one accepts the dating for the time of Artur, son of Aidan, our candidate for the historic Arthur, then this would reduce his age to a more acceptable hundred or so years.

Aneirin, son of Caw of Pryden and last of the ancient Bards produced as his principal work the description of the heroic battle of Catreath *c.* 599/600 in 'The Gododdin', where the war bands of Mynyddog Mwynfawr, Brythons of Dinas Eidin, sally forth to do battle with the foreign invaders. Although hopelessly outnumbered, they die as Heroes, inflicting great slaughter among their enemy.

One version of the poem states that only one man and the poet escape death to return to Dinas Eidin. In another version three men and the poet escape, but Kynon, son of Clydno Eidyn, definitely escapes in both versions. Kynon, brother to Euronwy and Creirwy, is said to have been extremely fond of his sister Euronwy, moving to Rheged after the battle to be near her, and is believed to have died later in Galloway, and to be buried there.

This poem is the oldest Scottish or, more correctly, Northern British poem, and one of the earliest to mention a person called Arthur, who was probably killed some eighteen years prior to this battle. It is significant that, in a long and many-versed poem, there is only one single mention of Arthur, suggesting he was a minor Hero of the north. There are a number of the named heroes at this battle that can be identified in the genealogia of Nennius.

The important point is that Aidan Mac Gabhran knew and soldiered alongside Myrddin at Arftyrydd; he no doubt recounted this to his children including Artur, and that is probably how Myrddin or Geoffrey of Monmouth's Merlin got into the mediaeval tales. He is most certainly associated with Artur's father Aidan, and through him to Artur himself.

CHAPTER 11
GEOFFREY OF MONMOUTH, HENRY OF HUNTINGDON AND WILLIAM OF MALMESBURY

Little is known of the early life of Geoffrey Arthur, alias Geoffrey of Monmouth, author of *The History of the Kings of Britain*. He is a Welsh cleric of Breton origin, whose family probably accompanied the Norman invasion. He is definitely a scholar and held the title of Master.

He may have been a Canon of the college of St George's in the church of Oxford Castle and he was friendly with Walter of Oxford, Archdeacon of the city, also with Robert of Chesney, Bishop of Lincoln. These men seem to have been his mentors during the time he wrote his history, which he claims was derived from an ancient book of the Britons in the possession of his friend Walter of Oxford.

This ancient book, which has not survived, was apparently written in the Britonic language, which he admitted he was not terribly familiar with. It is the basis of his work, together with Nennius's *Historia Brittonum*, and from these two principal works he concocted a story that did not disagree in general with what was already known, from Gildas through Bede to Nennius.

This history contains much on a 'King' Arthur, based on the revelations of Nennius about a long-forgotten hero of the Britons. It became the basis of the many works that were to follow, but particularly the romances of mediaeval times, written in the twelfth and thirteenth centuries. From that time on, the legends of Arthur have continued to flourish.

Geoffrey was very ambitious for a career in the Church, and his writings were all to that end. His first work was *The Prophecies of Merlin*, which was later incorporated into his main work, in which he takes Nennius's reference to an old bardic verse, describing the exploits of an ancient hero of the Britons who fights some twelve battles against invading Saesons or Saxons. This Hero's name was Arthur and he won all his battles, bringing a number of years of peace to his territory.

Nennius describes him as a War Leader, but Geoffrey for some reason or other makes him not just a King but a Super-King. He apparently was determined to give the ancient Britons of this country a history that they could be proud of and, using his imagination, described this King's other achievements in the way of his time, as indeed did the later romantic storytellers of mediaeval times.

Geoffrey took the lineage of the Britons right back to a Brutus, a leader of the Trojans, his founder of the nation, in the twelfth century BC, through biblical times to late seventh century AD.

He incorporates a magician called Merlin, based unfortunately on two different historical persons. One was Emrys of Carthmarthen in Wales, a Chief Druid of the fifth century, and the second Myrddin, a Chief Druid of the Selgovae tribe in southern Scotland, in the sixth century. *He named his mixed up character, Merlin.* This particular error, among others, later brought about many criticisms of his history, and eventually ridicule as a serious historian.

This was not for a considerable number of centuries, and even today many who study Arthurian historicity still find in Geoffrey's work much of which they consider relevant. However, in general most of his story is discredited as far as acceptable history is concerned.

It was, when first published, a 'best seller'. It came to the notice of

Henry of Huntingdon, a land-owner of some real prominence and a considerable historian himself, author of *Historia Anglorum*, who took it up as the virtual truth. He gave it his unqualified support, and in this guise it remained for a number of centuries the definitive work on the history of the British people.

There were some who disputed its veracity, namely William of Newburgh, who claimed it was all rubbish in the introduction to his own work *Historia Rerum Anglicarum*.

William of Malmesbury, probably the most able historian of the period, on the other hand, appears to accept the historical authenticity of an Arthur, and says, 'This is that Arthur of whom the Britons even at this day speak so idly: a man right worthy to have been celebrated by true story, not false tales; seeing it was he that long time upheld his declining country, even inspired martial courage into his countrymen.' He seems dubious of the tales then current on Artur, tales that Geoffrey of Monmouth probably made use of and included in his history, fabulising Nennius's simple poem or verses on a minor hero of the sixth century, into his 'King ' Artur.

William does not deny the historicity of Artur, but is not amused by people like Geoffrey who fabulised the story. He stops short however of denying them. He does state honestly, especially about the battle of Mons Badonicus as described by Gildas (which Geoffrey had virtually copied verbatim in his work), that since there is no mention of an Artur by Gildas at this battle, if, as Geoffrey and Nennius claim, it is Artur's last battle, then Artur must have been a senior officer, if not deputy to Ambrosius, who is the one accredited as leader and victor by Gildas.

This was the only solution that could make any sense of the battle of Mons Badonicus to William of Malmesbury. It was his simplification of an enigma that has been taken by later historians as proof of William's support of Geoffrey of Monmouth's statements on Artur, whereas he was only stating the obvious. If Geoffrey's story was true, since Gildas and Geoffrey of Monmouth give different victors to the battle, then Geoffrey's victor must at least have been a senior officer or even deputy to Gildas's victor.

Gildas was born in the year of the fight, which would therefore be well known to his parents and so to him. In other words, he was virtually contemporary with the battle, and is more likely to be correct in what he says than Geoffrey, writing almost six hundred years after the actual event.

William of Malmesbury does not support the view that Artur was victor at Mons Badonicus; he merely tries to come up with a solution to two differing versions of the battle, one almost contemporary, the other with claims made some five hundred plus years later.

It has to be remembered that in those days wizardry and witchcraft were believed in. It was not until the eighteenth century that such beliefs were really discarded and removed from serious history, so William of Malmesbury, although wary of most of the magic, does not completely deny all of it. His scepticism however shows through.

Geoffrey stated that the Teutonic peoples who landed on the east coast of Britain, and who later became known as the Northumbrians, landed on every river mouth from the Humber right up to the Beauly Firth in northern Scotland capable of taking their boats. This statement is about the most accurate piece of history his work contains!

These people, whom the Saxons called Angles as they tended to call all non-Saxon Teutons, but who properly called themselves Inglis (singular Ingle), gave their name to Ingleland as spelt by the early map makers both of Florence (Inglaterra) and then the Nederlands (Ingleland), who were the principal cartographical nations of mediaeval times.

Geoffrey, in dealing with Artur, says that the Northumbrians controlled the coast from the river Humber northwards. Yet when his Artur brings them to battle, for some reason they are on the south bank of their River Humber territory, around Barton-on-Humber. After

Artur defeats them, they flee not northwards towards their own territory, but further south to Lincoln. This suggests that Artur is attacking them from the north.

Artur follows and again defeats them. Now they turn and flee many miles to the north, into the Caledonian Forest in Scotland (Albion); still Artur follows and once more he defeats them.

They now turn south again and flee several hundred miles to the south-west, to Tintagel Castle in Cornwall, instead of running a few miles to the east of the forest, to the ancient fortress of Tantallon Castle on the east coast of southern Scotland, just east of North Berwick, a more understandable action. Artur again, according to Geoffrey, follows all the way to Cornwall and defeats them, whereupon the Northumbrians escape hundreds of miles northwards, back to the Caledonian Forest.

They are again defeated and apparently rush several hundred miles back south to Bath, instead of a few miles to the water of Bath at Beith in Ayrshire (probably a corruption of Bath, named after the small stream nearby, on the west side of the Caledonian Forest), but according to Geoffrey, Artur defeats them at Bath, England.

They turn once again to the north, travel several hundred miles and cross over the River Clyde, and on to the banks of Loch Lomond; Artur is still following and once more defeats them, etc., etc., etc.!

These various figures of several hundred miles to the north, then to the south, zig-zagging several thousand miles in total up and down the country by Artur, whom Geoffrey places in Cornwall, means he must have had the best Pigeon Post Intelligence Service, as well as the best Pony Express Cavalry, to keep up with all these manoeuvrings.

If however one starts with the Northumbrians who had landed on the upper reaches of the River Forth, Eocha and Ebissa and their descendants, and then use a proper knowledge of the geography of southern Scotland, it does begin to make some real sense describing battles in and around the Caledonian Forest and in the Forth Clyde Valley, as described in Chapter 9.

Geoffrey, because of the success of his *History* and with the patronage of Henry of Huntingdon, did achieve his ambition to achieve recognition in Church circles, and was ordained Priest and consecrated Bishop of St Asaph in Wales.

It is difficult to understand why Geoffrey's genealogy of the Britons led back to a Brutus, when it is recognised that the name of Britain was given wrongly by the Roman historians, who mistook the correct name of the inhabitants' land, the Prytanic Isles, 'Ynys Pryden', inhabited by the Pryderi. They mistook the 'P' for a 'B', probably from the largest and friendliest tribe the Brigantes, and hence the Pritanic Isles became the Britanic Isles, occupied by Britons (Brigantes), and certainly had nothing to do with a Brutus.

When the magic is taken out, and the wrong identification of the geography of the Arthurian battles, there is little left of his story that can be given much credence, as far as genuine history is concerned.

CHAPTER 12

THE ANCIENT WELSH AND OTHER GENEALOGIES

These ancient family trees, giving the lineages of the principal families of the northern Britons and a few of the southern tribes, were based originally on the verbal traditions of the Bards, and were quoted in Nennius's *Historia Brittonum*, which contained much on the families of these northern peoples. They included the Regal families of the Northumbrians. All of these later clerics brought up to date, the last additions being around the end of the thirteenth century.

The tremendous advantage of these family lines is that genuine lineages can be built up over several generations, and by using known dates and allowing some thirty to thirty-five years per generation, reasonable dates can be assigned to any particular person.

In those days and into much later mediaeval times, it was extremely necessary to have a pedigree. Without a lineage you were a nobody and could not claim or own land, so genealogical information was of the utmost importance, to both men and women, as in the twelfth and thirteenth centuries much land was claimed through a female ancestor, the distaff side, again proving that the ancient Britons were matrilineal in their succession rites.

The Genealogies also contain a large number of female lines, over

114

two hundred. This too confirms that matrilineal succession was practised by the early Britons. (See Appendix II.)

The last vestiges of this practice were continued by the Caledones or, as they later became to be known, the Picts, right up into the ninth century, when they came under the influence of the Dalriadic Scots, as in the ninth century Kenneth Mac Alpine became King of Scots and Picts.

Attached to the Genealogies contained in *The Early Welsh Genealogical Tracts* are a number of 'Lives' or '*Bonneds*', primarily of the Saints, which give a substantial number of lineages. Others, like the Lives of the Men of Aeron or Arwyr (Ayrshire), give the early ancestors of the Britons in what became the British Kingdom of Strathclyde.

The *Bonneds* do not always agree with the general name list in *The Early Welsh Genealogical Tracts*. For example, Denew, daughter of Llewdun Llwydawc of Dinas Eidin, is shown in one *Bonned* to be wife to Urien of Rheged, in another to be the wife of his son Owain, and in a further one to be married to Gwrtheryn Gwrtheneu, father to Artur's wife Gwenwhyvawr! Nor does the genealogical information in the *Mabinogion* get much, if any, confirmation from the ancient Welsh name lists, which suggests there is something very wrong with the *Mabinogion* listings.

Perhaps 'the son of' means 'son of his mother', e.g., 'Peredur, son of Eurawc (his mother)'. Angharad Law Eurawc was lover to Peredur in his search for the Grail, and may have got confused with his mother.

One of the most important lineages is that for Artur, son of Uther Pendragon, as follows:

1. **Coel Hen Godebog**, father of Ceneu.
2. **Ceneu**, father of Gwrwst Ledlum.
3. **Gwrwst Ledlum**, father of Meirchion Gul.
4. **Meirchion Gul**, father of Elidir Lydanwyn.

5. **Elidir Lydanwyn**, father of Llywarch Hen.
6. **Llywarch Hen**, father of Madog.
7. **Madog**, father of Cynfor.
8. **Cynfor**, father of Custenin Fendigaid or Goreneu.
9. **Custenin Fendigaid** or **Goreneu**, father of Uther Pendragon.
10. **Uther Pendragon**, father of Arthur.

At some thirty-five years to a generation from the death of Coel Hen (*c.* 430), this would make this Arthur son of Uther, an early ninth century person! By this time Uther would have a knowledge of Nennius' best-seller, the *Historia Brittonum*, naming a heroic Arthur, and so would be able to name one of his sons Arthur after him.

Uther's castle is nowhere near Cornwall, but at Appleby-in-Westmorland in Cumbria. He was a descendant of the *Gwyr Y Gogledd*, a 'Man of the North'.

The presently accepted genealogy on the other hand is as follows:

Arthur, son of Uther Pendragon, son of Custenin (Note *not* Custenin Fendigaid), son of Maxen Weldig, and so jumps several generations to make Arthur a late fifth or early sixth century person. It is doubtful if the Roman general Maximus (Macsen Weldig) who used British legions to seize the Emperorship, ever married a woman of the Britons! He is supposed to have married Elen Lwddog, daughter of Eudaf, but the ancient genealogies show Elen Lwddog as the daughter of Coel (note, not Coel Hen Godebog). Modern historians do not necessarily confirm or, to be fair, deny the marriage, and there are many place-names in Wales remembering her, so it is a moot question.

Another important lineage is that of Cunneda Weldig, as follows:

1. **Cunneda Weldig**, son of Eydern.
2. **Eydern**, son of Pedwrn or Padarn.
3. **Pedwrn** or **Padarn**, son of Gwynnog.
4. **Gwynnog** son of Coel Hen Godebog.

This makes Cunneda an early sixth century personage.

There is a slight problem in that a daughter of Coel, Gwal, is shown as both Cunneda's mother and his wife! This can be overcome as the Coel listed is not given *generally* as Coel Hen Godebog, and so Gwal is probably a sister to Elen Lwddog, daughter of this other Coel. The *Bonned Y Sant* (Note 7), quotes Gwal as a daughter of Coel Hen, and is the only one to do so, but this is believed to be an error.

This is an example where one has to be careful in dealing with similar names.

The most important lineages affecting this story are those of the *Bonedd Gwyr Y Gogledd*, the lives of the Men of the North:

1. **Urien** of Rheged, son of Cynfarch O'Oer, descended from Coel Hen.

    He was one of the most powerful British Chiefs, quoted as the Pillar of Britain, called in the Arthurian Romances Urien of Gorre, and shown as an adversary of Artur in the tales. Our version of Artur's relationship with Urien however is that Artur was indeed a friend to him, as was his father Aidan.

    Urien did lead his tribe with other British tribes against the Northumbrians, assisted by Llywarch Hen, Guallawc, Dunawt and possibly Geraint, son of Erbin, driving them off the mainland on to the Farne Islands.

    Unfortunately his second-in-command was Modred, son of Low or Loth of Lothian, who in jealousy had Urien assassinated at Aber Llew, mouth of the River Low, just north of Bambro' Castle. This led to the breaking up of the alliance of tribes, thus allowing the Northumbrians back to the mainland, later to take their revenge.

    His Bard Taliesin never ceased to sing his praises. He is described as 'Lord of the cultivated plain', showing that warfare was not his only occupation, but that agriculture was important to the tribe.

2. **Llywarch Hen**, son of Elider Lydanwyn, descended from Coel Hen.

He was a warrior Bard of the Britons, and his cousin Loth of Lothian placed him as Bard in his most southerly fortress of Dinguaroy, which became Bambro' Castle. This was the first British coastal fort in the northern part of the land to be captured by the Northumbrians, by Ida of Bernicia in *c*. 557.

Llywarch Hen must have put up a spirited resistance as he is quoted as one of the Heroic Men of the North. He had to retreat, surprisingly, not to his cousin and mentor Loth in the north, nor to his other heroic and favoured relation Urien in the west, but instead, made his way south-west to Powys in Wales. This can only be explained by realising that the Chief in Powys was Cynddylan, one of his many sons.

This Cynddylan is often shown, wrongly, as a son of Cyndrwyn, but in the *Bonedd yr Arwyr*, item 1, which gives the sons of Kyndrwyn, there is no mention of a Cynddylan. In item 5, however, which gives the children of Llywarch Hen, child number 27 is Kynddylan. Hence Llywarch's actions confirm him as father to Cynddylan. (Note the letters 'C' and 'K' are interchangeable.)

Stand out maids, and look on the land of Cynddylan,
The court of Pengwern is ablaze; alas for the young who mourn
their brothers...
The hall of Cynddylan is dark tonight,
Without fire, without bed; I weep awhile and then fall silent...

The following is taken from *Old Houses of Shrewsbury* by H.E. Forest (1932):

The earliest mention of any house in Shrewsbury occurs in the writings of Llywarch Hen, the British poet who is supposed to have lived about the end of the sixth century (critics aver that the poem was actually written in late Saxon times, but even if this were so, it would have some historic value, as recording traditions that were generally accredited then). He came from Northumbria (Dinguroy later Bebba's or Bambro' Castle), to take refuge with Cynddylan, Prince of Powys, the last British Chief to rule east of the Severn, whose home was at Pengwern, the British Shrewsbury.

The poet laments the destruction of Viroconium and of Pengwern, 'whose maidens he bids to behold the habitation of Cynddylan wrapted in flames'. Probably Pengwern was not wholly destroyed then: at any rate it was soon reoccupied for in *c.* 606 Brochmael, Prince of Powys had his palace there on the site subsequently occupied by old St Chad's church.

Soon afterwards the Saxons took possession of the town which became part of Mercia and was first called Scrobbesbyrig, this name by a series of mutations taking its modern form, Shrewsbury.

3. **Clydno Eidyn** son of Cenfelyn, descended from Coel Hen.

He is one of the Heroic Men of the North and hence a powerful Chieftain, whose lands lay at Caer Eidyn at the eastern end of the Antonine Wall, modern day Carriden, Bo'ness. It is suggested that his daughter Creirwy became wife to Aidan Mac Gabhran, and this because of the British way of matrilineal succession brought him lands in Slammanan, i.e., Camelon and Avolond. She was Artur's mother.

4. **Dunawt** son of Cerwyd, descended from Coel Hen.

Little is known of this Dunawt, other than that he is affirmed in the ancient genealogies and is of the family of Pabo Post Pryden, indeed is his grandson.

He could be a candidate for 'Dunawt the Stout' instead of the son of Cynan Garwyn (whom we think would be rather young in *c.* 574) who assisted Peredur and Gwrgi at the battle of Arftyrydd. He is associated with Llywarch Hen.

5. **Gwrgi** son of Eliffer Gosgordfawr, descended from Coel Hen.

He was the younger brother of Peredur, he of the steel weapons. Their mother was Madrun, daughter of Gwrtheyrn Gwrtheneu and sister to Artur's wife, Gwenwhyvawr.

6. **Gwendalleau** son of Cedio, descended from Coel Hen.

He was cousin to Creirwy, Aidan's wife. This relationship brought Aidan into the battle of Arftyrydd, supporting Gwendalleau, who was now Chief of the Selgovae tribe, it is thought through matrilineal succession. This marriage did not seem popular with his in-laws, the family of Cynfarch O'Oer, who left him on his own at the battle of Arftyrydd.

He and the father of Myrddin, his Chief Druid, one Morken, were killed there.

7. **Trychan Cledyf Kynverchyn?**

It is difficult to give much information on this person, as his name under this spelling does not appear in the general name list in the ancient genealogies but in the *Bonedd Gwyr Y Gogledd*. However he could appear as Kynvelyn or Cunobelinus of Edinburgh. (See Dr John Morris: *Age of Arthur*, p. 215 and the *Bonedd Gwyr Y Gogledd*.) There are a number of Kynvelyn or Cynfelyns, and Cledyf seems to be a descriptive name meaning sword, hence Trychan the sword of Kynfelyn, to differentiate him from others of this name.

8. **Ryderych Hael** son of Tutwal Tudclyd, son of Clynog (Cedig or Ceredig) descended from Coel Hen.

He was probably the most famous of the northern Britons, after Urien of Rheged, defeating Aidan and Gwendalleau at Arftyrydd.

He expanded the British tribal lands of Alcluyd into the largish British conglomerate of Strathclyde. The Britons of the area continued to use the name of Britons right into the eleventh century, when they became part of modern Scotland. The Selgovae tribe disappeared, apparently joining up with the Gotadinii, after Ryderych's victory at Arftyrydd.

9. **Mordaf** son of Serwan, descended from Coel Hen.

He was cousin to Ryderych Hael, so nephew to Tudwal Tutclyd. His aunt Gwasawc married Morken or Mourig of the Selgovae, who fathered Myrddin who became Chief Druid of that tribe.

10. **Elfin** son of Gwyddno, descended from Coel Hen.

This person is seventh in descent from Coel Hen and therefore one of the youngest Men of the North, and apparently of an age with Artur. Which battle or battles earned him the right to be a member of the Heroic *Gwyr Y Gogledd* can only be surmised.

11. **Guaran**, descended from Macsen Weldig.

It is difficult to agree Guaran's pedigree, as after tracing it back to Dyfnwal Hen, instead of then taking it back to Coel Hen, as a Man of the North, the *Bonedd* takes his lineage via a different Dyfnwal Hen (usually spelt Dinual) back to Macsen Weldig.

12. **Elidyr Mwynvawr**, son of Gwrwst Briodor, descended from Coel Hen.

He was closely related to Ryderych Hael, whose father and Elidyr Mwynvawr's grandfather were brothers, so they are second cousins, probably supporting Ryderych in all his battles.

13. **Huall**, descended from Amlawt Weldig.

He appears to have been either a Cornishman who lived in the north or from a northern branch of the Cornovii.

Artur is contemporary with most of the Men of the North's sons, and like Owain, son of Urien, got his exploits tacked on to the end of the *Gwyr Y Gogledd* sagas.

Listed below is the family tree of Artur's wife Gwenwhyvawr.

1. **Gwenwhyvaur**, daughter of Gwrtheyrn Gwrtheneu.
2. **Gwrtheyrn Gwrtheneu**, son of Gwyddol.
3. **Gwyddol**, son of Dyfnwal Hen.
4. **Dyfnwal Hen**, son of Gorwynion.
5. **Gorwynion**, son of Ceneu.
6. **Ceneu**, son of Coel Hen Godebog.

The name Gwrtheyrn Gwrtheneu is interesting as it is derived from Gurthrigerno, or Vortigern, meaning High Chief. The usage of the name confirms the colony of Cornovii, who used this title, in Rheged in Galloway, where obviously he, though a descendant of Coel Hen, had through his maternal side descent from the Cornovii tribe and a claim to its Chieftaincy.

In creating a genealogical tree of the descendants of Coel Hen Godebog, first through eight generations, then, after the Northumbrians over-ran Rheged when a number of his descendants returned to unconquered Wales, continuing their lines through some thirty plus generations (unfortunately too large to incorporate in this book) a number of decisions had to be made in respect to anomalies in the genealogies.

The principal one was in respect of Dyfnwal (Hen), often quoted as the begetter of the Men of the North. He is shown as having a father Gorbanion or Garbanion or Gorwynion, but if these three are one and the same person, then not only did he have a son Dyfnwal (Hen), but a second son of the same name, Dyfnwal (Molemut). It was unheard of, even with twins (except in Ireland), to call two sons both with the same name, in this case Dyfnwal. The descriptive appendages of Hen (the old or wise) and Molemut (split lip), would be ascribed to them in later life. Hence the conclusion was reached that Gorwynion was a separate person from the other two whose names are so familiar, with only one letter different, and so parent to one of the Dyfnwals.

Indeed, when one extracts the names from the Ancient Welsh Tracts for the preparation of Coel Hen's genealogical tree, Gorwynion son of Ceneu lends himself as the parent of Dyfnwal Hen, and so sorts this out.

Unfortunately there are two Dyfnwal Hens, the one from the north always spelt 'Dyfnwal' and the other or southern one, often spelt 'Dinwal' or 'Dinual'.

Dyfnwal Molemut was the High Chief who gave the Cumbrians or North British their basic laws.

Other decisions concern the numerous names that are the same, and the ones used have been considered over the years by trial and error, until a satisfactory lineage was arrived at. Cenfelyn or Cynfelyn is one of these names, and there are others. However the present relationships in general all appear to fall into their correct families.

It is interesting how most of the clans are related through marriage. Artur's lineage on his Iro-Scots side is as follows:

Echach Muinremair father of Ercc, of the Ui Neil.
Ercc father of Fergus.
Fergus father of Gabhran.
Gabhran father of Aidan.
Aidan father of Artur. (See Table 2).

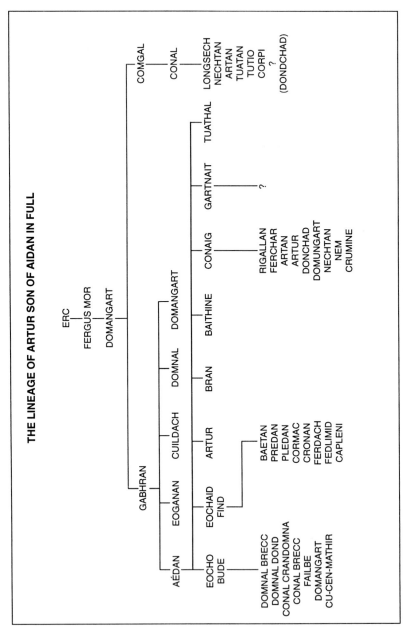

Table 2

His line through his mother on his Brythonic side is:

Creirwy his mother, daughter of Clydno Eidyn.
Clydno Eidyn son of Cynfelyn.
Cynfelyn son of Arthrwys.
Arthrwys son of Mar or Maes Gloff.
Mar or **Maes Gloff** son of Ceneu.
Ceneu son of Coel Hen Godebog.

It is a fascinating study on its own, working out the relationships of these people who lived almost 1,500 years ago, in a time known as the 'Dark Ages'. It is particularly interesting how many of the tribes were interrelated by marriage, and more so in matrilineal marriages, showing an amazing freedom of travel and exchange of information between tribes in these early days.

We would have liked to have expanded this compilation to include where possible the wives and daughters, but it was becoming very unwieldy. Any more names would have made it more difficult to follow and read, and so we have the female names as Appendix II.

In Appendix III, we have listed the contemporaries of Artur, those names that are sixth in descent from Coel Hen Godebog.

CHAPTER 13
A BACKGROUND TO ARTUR
AND HIS CONTEMPORARIES

Without going all the way back to Coel Hen Godebog, we would like to start our background by considering the tribe of the Selgovae in the latter half of the fifth century. They were then led by Meirchion Gul, father of Cynfarch O'Oer. Meirchion is described in early scripts as the 'Admiral of the Fleet' of the Britons in the east, where their galleys were based on the Firth of Forth.

This suggests that the Mannawins of Mannu Gododdin, the Gotadini or Gododdin and the Selgovae, all had mutual defensive treaties and that by their joint consent, the sailor Chief Meirchion Gul became their fleet commander.

An alternative theory is that the lands of the Selgovae in the east reached the coast of the Firth of Forth, physically dividing the north and south Gododdin tribes (Mannau Goddin and the Gododdin), giving the Selgovae direct access to the sea around Portobello or Musselborough. In this case, it is likely that Meirchion Gul resided in the Clan's most easterly fort of Tinnis Castle, some thirty miles from the coast, or even at his grandson's Hall of Trapain Law, only some ten miles from the Forth estuary, leaving his son Cynfarch in charge of the main tribal seat of the Selgovae at Castle O'Oer.

After the battle of Arftyrydd, the Selgovae amalgamated with the Gododdin in the east, and south of Edinburgh are a number of places with decidedly Brythonic place names, like Penicuik (Pen Y Cuan –

Head of the Owl), and within its parish was Welsh Town (Welchtoune) or the village of Welsh or British speakers. This despite south-east Scotland being overrun by the Angles from the seventh century onwards.

Into this background, Aidan, son of Gabhran, through marriage became part of this amalgam of tribes and his daughter Gwyar married Meirchion Gul's grandson, Low or Loth of Lothian and the Gotadini. His son Artur took up, on his father's behalf, the defence of Camelon and Avalond as well as the guardianship of the eastern end of the Antonine Wall, so involving him in the politics of his relatives among these British tribes.

Apart from his immediate family, the most important person to affect Artur's young life would appear to be Urien of Rheged. If this presented hypothesis has any degree of truth to it, Artur finished learning the craft of a Warrior at Urien's hands, in his Hall at Caer Laverock Castle. It is there that he met his wife to be, daughter of one of Urien's chief advisors.

There is some controversy over the location of Urien's Hall, apart from our preferred location of Caer Laverock, derived from R.L. Graeme Ritchie's deductions.

One might put forward the Mote of Mark nearby, as well as Carlisle, Caer Llion, itself. This is doubtful, as in the sixth century Carlisle would have been a deserted and ruined Roman city, as described by Gildas and Bede. In fact, a biographer of St Cuthbert describes the saint visiting the ruins of Roman Carlisle in *c.* AD 685.

Even the ancient fortress of Dun Rheged, present day Dunraggit, in Galloway, could come into the reckoning as his residence.

Urien or Urbgen was the High Chief of the largest and most powerful British tribe, the amalgam of the Novantae, founded in Rheged, a land that seemed to stretch from Galloway through Dumfries, north into Ayrshire, then into the region of the Borders, crossing over the Hadrianic wall into Cumberland and Northumberland as far south possibly as Catterick.

Plate 3: Caer Laverock Castle and earliest mound
of the old fortification

Urien of Erchwydd,
Christendom's most generous man,
a myriad gifts
you gave
to the men of the world.

Taliesin

128

He was known as the Lord or Shepherd of Erechwydd, possibly Ercledoune, now Earlstoun, Berwickshire.

Dr Graham Webster in his book *The Cornovii* suggests that the Cornovii centred on Wroxeter were under the protection of Urien, so that his influence also covered Lancashire and spread into Powys in Wales.

Urien is described by his Bard, Taliesin, as the bravest and best loved of all the British Chiefs, the most powerful of the Men of the North, the *Gwyr Y Gogledd*. He reigned supreme from Galloway to perhaps Shropshire in the south-west, and as far as Catterick in the east.

Taliesin never ceased to sing the praises of Urien, and always finished up with the following:

> *Till I am old and failing*
> *In the grim doom of death*
> *I shall have no delight*
> *If my lips praise not Urien*

Urien achieved the same fame as Artur. He organised his neighbouring tribes and led them against Theodoric of Northumbria, whom he well and truly defeated, driving him into the sea and on to the Farne Isles, *c*. AD 590.

Unfortunately, Urien's second in command, his nephew Modred or Medraut, son of Low or Loth, was angered that Urien, in appreciation of help from Scots allies, gave these Scots Dinguaroy (Bambro' Castle), which was Modred's father Loth's most southerly fortress. Feeling slighted at this and jealous of Urien's success as a leader, he plotted and had Urien assassinated.

Urien's death broke up the alliance and the Britons departed to their own tribal territories, thus allowing the Northumbrians off the hook and back on to the mainland, to take their ultimate revenge later.

This was the eventual obliteration of the Britons, except for those in Devon, Cornwall, Wales and Strathclyde. Urien's sister Efrddyl, divorced wife of Ellifer Gosgordfawr, mourns him in the poetry of Llywarch Hen.

The *Bonned Y Sants* (Life of the Saints in the *Genealogical Tracts*) give Urien three wives, including Ethni, daughter of Alfryd, son of Grono, son of Gwydion, son of Don of these parts, and we suggest she was of the Carvetii tribe, giving Urien the title to the Chieftaincy of the conglomerate, the Novantae. His other wives were Euronwy, daughter of Clydno Eidyn, sister to Creirwy, and Denew, daughter of Lewdwyn Luydawc of Dinas Eidin. The latter two names can be placed geographically in Mannu Gododdin, leaving Ethni as possibly his first wife and her father Alfryd who gave him the Chieftaincy of Rheged through matrilineal succession, as very little is known about them.

There is no evidence whatsoever that Rheged was ever formed by warfare or coercion of any sort, least of all by Urien.

One of Urien's most telling battles was fought against the Northumbrians under Aethelric who invaded Rheged, demanding hostages, but it is claimed that Urien and his son Owain beat him on 'a Saturday morning in Argoed Llwyfein', Leven Forest, which location suggests the River Leven which flows out of Loch Lomond or, alternatively, a Leven Forest in Cumbria or Northumbria, the location of which has got lost.

Urien's son Owain would be of an age with Artur and, like their fathers, the boys might have been good friends from his sojourns at Caer Laverock.

Owain was attacked by Fflamddwyn (Flame-bearer or Firebrand):

> *Fflamddwyn hollered*
> *with great commotion,*
> *– Have my hostages come,*
> *are they ready?*

And answered Owain,
– They haven't come,
they don't exist,
they aren't ready

Taliesin

Owain killed and defeated him, but it was the beginning of the end of the Heroic age.

Owain was honour bound to avenge his father's assassination, thus forcing the Britons to quarrel among themselves, which was a recipe for disaster. He was killed in battle against Dunaut the Fierce or Stout, Guallauc, Morcant (Modred) and Bran, at an unknown location and with him died the land and Chieftaincy of Rheged.

Within two or three decades, the Inglis would have overrun both Owain's and Artur's fortresses or halls. They were the last of the *Gwyr Y Gogledd*, sons of the Heroes of the North.

When Owain killed Flamddwyn
It was no more
to him
than to sleep.
The great host of Lloegr
sleep
With a glaze in their eyes
And those who didn't flee
a little way
were braver than was need.

Owain was known as Caesarius: Owain the Caesar of the North, suggesting that some Roman titles were still known and in use in Albion, or at least knowledge survived of the Roman occupation.

Artur's uncle Kynon, his mother's brother, the only definite one to escape death at the battle of Catreath, son of one of the thirteen Heroic Men of the North, was obviously a warrior extraordinary to survive that battle. This shows a young Artur surrounded by fighting men of great worth. When it came Artur's time he followed their heroic example, so gaining a warrior's reward, a saga of his exploits in the metre of the British Bards.

Unfortunately, on his warrior father's side, his exploits were only what his father Aidan would have expected of him, or indeed any other son, and so he was not looked upon as a hero in Dalriadic circles: they were all brave warriors to each other!

The large family of Llwyarch Hen, of which only three names are given in our genealogy, are all contemporaries of our Arthur, similarly with the sons of Caw of Pryden. (See Appendix IV.)

CHAPTER 14
LATER HISTORIANS

It was not until the nineteenth century that meaningful historic investigations were properly undertaken, looking, as W.F. Skene put it, at the most contemporary historians with Artur and then subjecting them to rigorous examination. With this method, Skene brought new insights on to where to look for early British history: in the ancient Books of Wales, which intersected with the time of Artur. Skene therefore laid a foundation for such studies that cannot be improved upon even to this day. That is not to say that he got everything right, but he showed the way. He had to rely on modern Welsh speakers to translate early Welsh Bardic verse written in 'Old' Welsh, telling of ancient battles, never shying away from a defeat but praising always bravery, be it in victory or adversity. Some of the translations that he received were not, with hindsight, particularly good.

As far as Artur goes, Skene's investigations into the battle of Arftyrydd, and his identification of the site at the Knowles of Arthuret, north-east of Carlisle, near Carwinnley (Caer Gwendalleau), and the Mote and Baillies of Liddel, with the peoples involved and the outcome, are crucial to the background to a historic Artur. His other great contribution was his identification of the majority of the Arthurian battle sites, as described by Nennius. His books are quite difficult to come by, and we have to thank the local library at Loanhead for the efforts made in obtaining some of his works for us.

Contemporary with Skene was the antiquarian Stuart Glennie,

whose method of identifying 'Scottish' Arturian sites was to walk over the actual ground and listen to local legend, then to see if the two would support one another. His locations for Artur's twelve battles are more precise than Skene's, and are therefore to be preferred. His sites for the battles were:

1) At the River or Water of Glen at its junction with the River Irvine in the Parish of Loudon, Ayrshire.

2) At the mouth of the River Leven in Alcluyd (Dumbarton).

3), 4) and 5) all on the rivers and glen named Dubglas (Douglas), at Loch Lomond in Lennox (Linneas).

6) On the river of the Bassas (*bass* singular, *bassas* plural), which word means a conical hill looking as if man-made but actually a natural rock formation, e.g., the Bass Rock in the Firth of Forth. He identifies the two conical hills at Dunipace, Stirlingshire, as the Bassas referred to, and the river flowing past them is the Bonny.

7) The battle of Cat Coit Celeddon (battle of the Caledon Wood), he locates in either the forest of Selkirk or the forest of Ettrick.

8) Castle Guinnion or Garanwynyon, a Roman fort surveyed by General Roy around 1770, described by Taliesin as the site of the battle of Gwenystrad, in the old district of Wedale, in English or old Saxon Woe-dale, the Dale of Woe; Latin *Vallis Doloris* around Stow (anciently Stow in Wedale), sometimes mistaken for Wensleydale in England.

Here Taliesin reports on Urien being involved, and makes the first mention of any of the Chiefs supporting Artur. (See page 105.)

In defending Gwenystrad was seen
A mound and slanting ground obstructing...
Hand on the cross they wail on the gravel bank of Garanwynyon.

9) Nennius' Kaer Lium, identified as Dumbarton, *'Castle Arthuri'*.

10) Tratheu Trywruid or Carse of Stirling.

11) Mont Agned or Arthur's Seat, Edinburgh.

12) Bowden Hill or Buden Hill, a few miles south-east of Camelon.

At this time Lady Charlotte Guest published in Saxon English the Welsh Arthurian stories, under the general title *The Mabinogion*. Unfortunately the many names and family trees quoted in these stories do not in general gain much confirmation from Nennius's *Genealogies* of the Britons.

Coming into the twentieth century, there is a wealth of historical works concerning Artur and his location, all with some degree of argument for this area or that.

Among the earliest to mention Artur is the Rev. A.B. Scott, in his history of *The Pictish Nation, its People and its Church*. It is ostensibly a history of the Celtic Church as practised by St Ninnian of Candida Cassa and his missionary work in the early spread of Christianity throughout Britain and the Northern Isles. This was at the end of the fourth century and into the fifth and sixth. He describes how it was affected by the creation of Dalriada and the Ionian Church by the Scots from Ireland. He equates the Picts as the Northern Britons, and mentions a minor or petty King called Arthur based around Stirling in the sixth century.

He gives the early Pictish King Lists, with a very acceptable dating, but is not often read or quoted today. He states that Arthur was one of the thirteen named Men of the North, which we cannot accept as these Men of the North are named in the *Bonned Gwyr Y Gogledd* and most are Artur's elders. (See Chapter 12.)

One of the most prolific Arthurian researchers is Professor Norma L. Goodrich, and in the many editions of her book *King Arthur*, she takes the Fables and makes a history out of them, including the search for the Holy Grail and other later additions to the stories. She is, however, convinced Artur should be placed in southern Scotland. She quotes two lineages for Artur – one of Uther Pendragon coupling with Ygerne, wife of Gorlois and begetting Artur under the magic of Merlin (taken from the *Morte d'Arthur*). The other line she uses descends from Cunedda Weldig.

We argue that Artur, son of Uther Pendragon, is in fact an early ninth-century person, not to be confused with a sixth-century Artur.

She repeats the story where Urien (of Gorre) abducts Gwenevere, whereas we have shown via the genealogies that Gwenevere was indeed at Urien of Rheged's Hall, but not as a captive or abductee. She was a daughter of one of his advisers, Gwrtheyrn Gwrtheneu. She was sister to Madrun, who became a second wife to Eliffer Gosgordfawr of Elmet.

Professor Goodrich, with R.L. Graeme Ritchie, believes that Artur was born at Caer Laverock Castle, and that it was the home of his mother.

Our hypothesis is that Artur had his Warrior's education completed there under Urien's tutelage and that while there, he met and married Gwenwhyvawr, making Caer Laverock his mother-in-law's home. This explanation, we feel, is much more likely.

Her locations for his twelve battles differ in some degree to the Skene/Glennie locations which we mostly prefer. In particular, the Binchester location propounded by K.H. Jackson that she adopts is too far south for battles or skirmishes in and around the Forth-Clyde Valley and Caledon Wood in Scotland, as our premise suggests. S. Glennie has Cat Coit Cleydon (battle of Caledon Wood) in the area of Ettrick or Selkirk forests, both quite far south on the Scottish Borders.

One would have liked to include Sir Lancelot Du Lac of Écosse (Scotland), of whom Professor Goodrich gives a lineage as a son of King Ban of Benoic, but since the ancient genealogies do not confirm such a person, sadly he has been discarded in our historical sense.

Similarly, she names the three sons of Cynfarch O'Oer, as Urien of Rheged, Low or Loth of Lothian, and Anguselus (a King Lancelot). This last person is not confirmed in the ancient genealogies, which show a third son named Anwrad, and so we have, with some misgivings discarded Anguselus.

None the less, her work on Arthur is monumental, particularly her identification of places described in the Romances, and is an essential text for all Arthurian interpreters.

Another prolific historian was the late Dr John Morris. His important work *The Age of Arthur* is a mine of information on early British history, gleaned from early Welsh sources, out-stripping Skene in this sphere. It was unfortunate that he died before he was able to finish his investigations into Nennius's work. He did not place Artur in Scotland, but in the south-west of England, and his locations for Rheged are, we feel, far too far south into England as far as his Map 13 is concerned, but he corrects this impression in his text. His other important works are *Londonium* and *British History and the Welsh Annals* (Phillimore 1980).

Two other writers are Geofrey Ashe and Professor Leslie Alcock, an archaeologist favouring the claims of English Cadbury and Glastonbury. Both are members of the Camelot Research Committee and are responsible for numerous Arthurian books.

Professor Alcock says, '...unfortunately, that the use of primitive and old Welsh verse as a historic source is not so simple as this might suggest; for a start not all the poems which praise the martial valour of British heroes were composed, to be recited in their presence, some of them are actually elegies of long dead heroes.'! This we feel does not necessarily exclude them as a source of history.

On the early history of the founding of the Iro-Scots colony of Dalriada and its relationship with the neighbouring territories, there can be no better investigative work than Dr John Bannerman's *Studies in the History of Dalriada*, based on the many Scottish or northern references in the Irish Annals, but primarily on Adamnan's *Life of Columba* and the *Senchus Fer nAlban* (History of the Scots), both based on seventh century documents.

Dr Bannerman prefers Artur to be a grandson of Aidan, as suggested by the Senchus, whilst we prefer Adomnan's identification of him as a son of Aidan. Much on Aidan's life that we use is derived from this work.

Dr Richard Barber, through the Boydell Press, has produced a number of books on the Arthurian Romances, and one in particular on the historic person of Arthur titled *The Figure of Arthur*, in which he argues that there were in the sixth century two Arthurs, one in Dalriada in the north, son of Aidan son of Gabhran, and one, son of Reithoir or Pedr in the south in Dyfed, descended from the Dessi tribe or Crimthan of Ireland. In a scholarly exposition he puts the case for the Dalriadic Arthur as the historic candidate. His work on Gildas and on the Welsh Triads are particularly enlightening. His latest books, *King Arthur* and *The Arthurian Legends*, are all very understandable statements on the early sources for the deduction of a historic Arthur.

We hope that our views on Artur, son of Aidan, sit reasonably well on Dr Barber's solid foundation, reviving an interest in the *Gwyr Y Gogledd*, the Britons or *Cymry* and others in the north.

N. Tolstoy's book *The Quest for Merlin* is the best work we know on Merlin. His description of the battle of Arftyrydd is a marvellous scenario of which we have made full use.

We do differ, however, in our identification of the Hart Fell that Merlin fled to in his escape from the field of Arftyrydd; the Hart Fell above the town of Moffat is too far north into his enemy Ryderych's lands and therefore far too hazardous for him to visit from there, to Hoddam in the south, where he met up with St Kentigern.

This is why we have identified Hart Fell in the forest and lands of

Castle O'Oer. This would give him some protection from his kinsman Cynfarch, and a considerably shorter journey to flee to from the field of Arftyrydd, and easy to visit to Hoddama Cross, by descending from Hart Fell via the Bottom Burn to the junction with the Water of Milk. From there is but a short journey to its confluence with the River Annan and so to Hoddam Cross, where Kentigern was Priest.

P.K. Ford's book on the *Poetry of Llywarch Hen* (University of California Press) is an excellent exposition on this warrior bard.

Recently, a new book, *King Arthur, the True Story*, by Graham Philips and Martin Keatman, claims that a little known chief in Powys, Owain Dangwyn, son of Einion Yrth, son of Cunneda Weldig, is the true King Arthur. However despite their deductions, it is what they leave out of their story that argues against their conclusions. Obviously, whilst admiring their book's lucidity, we do not concur with many of their tenets.

For example, they believe that in the sixth century, there were no Britons north of Hadrian's Wall, only Picts, even though that edifice divided the largest British tribe, the Brigantes, into two parts, a large part of their territory occupying much of southern Scotland, north of the Wall.

Similarly with the Carvetii tribe, whose lands were around the eastern end of the Solway firth from say Gretna Green to well south of the Wall well beyond Carlisle. These cut-off peoples did not cease to be British and become Picts, because of a man made boundary!

We would also push the case for the Strathclyde Britons, occupying the tribal lands of the Damnonii or Dumnonii, who remained unconquered by the English, Irish or Scots until they joined the embryonic Kingdom of Scotland early in the eleventh century, retaining the ancient name of Britons to that date and beyond.

In a charter in 1164 Malcolm IV of Scotland, addressed them separately, as 'Normans, Saxons, Scots, Welsh (Strathclyde Britons) and Picts'.

As late as the year 1297, the lines above the old Stirling bridge across the Forth read:

I am free march, as passengers may ken,
To Scots, to Britons, and to Inglis men.

A seventeenth century poem says:

From Penryn Weleth [Glasgow] *to Loch Reon* [Ryan]
The Cymri are of one mind, bold heroes.

The heir to the Scottish Kingdom, David son of Malcolm III (Canmore) was 'Prince of Cumbria' (Strathclyde), in the way that male heirs of the present throne are titled 'Prince of Wales' today. See G. Eyre Todd's *The Story of Glasgow.*

Even the earliest Northern British or Scottish poem 'The Gododdin' by Aneirin, states that Mynyddog Mwynfawr of Dinas Eidin with his British war bands were 'Brythons' and most certainly of the northern Votadinii, hence a British tribe. Therefore Cunedda and his family of the Gododdin were northern Britons, speaking 'P' Celtic, and not, as they suggest, foreigners.

In fact if we look at the four ancient Bards of the Welsh (British), Taliesin, Llywarch Hen, Myrddin and Aneirin, three of them are Britons born in the land of Pryden, Albion or Yscotlant, north of Hadrian's Wall: Llywarch Hen, son of Elider Lydanwyn, brother to Cynfarch O'Oer of the Selgovae; Myrddin, son of Morken, Chief of the Alcluyd Britons, who became Chief Druid, Bard and advisor to the Selgovae tribe; and Aneirin, son of Caw of Pryden in the lands of the Damnonii or Dumnonii (Renfrewshire). Lastly comes Taliesin. His birth is shrouded in mysticism, but he was Chief Bard in the Hall of Urien of Rheged, certainly in the north.

Philips and Keatman maintain a belief that Urien's land of Rheged is wholly south of Hadrian's Wall, when indeed it was largely made up of Galloway and Dumfries, north of the Wall, extending into Cumbria, a British name used to describe the land right up to the River Clyde (and is the northern dialect for Cambria) and part of Northumbria. Its name was derived from Dun Rheged, present day Dunraggit in Galloway.

The authors examining geographical places associated with Artur in Britain seem to stop at the Hadrian Wall, as the most northerly point of the British Isles! All northern Cymric and Arthurian references in Scotland, of which there are many, are ignored.

At that time, i.e., before Cunedda moved to Wales, much of the western half of modern Wales was occupied by the 'Gwyddel' or Irish Gaels, the Britons (Welsh) having eastern Wales and western England, whilst in eastern England the Teutonic tribes, in the sixth century, predominated. North of Hadrian's Wall, in the Rhins of Galloway, were Irish Cruithne or Picts, along with the northern Cymry, who spread into central southern Scotland with Angles in the south-east and Britons with mixed Britons and Caledons, the Brythwyr (Speckled ones or Brito-Picts) round the east end of the Antonine Wall, in Mannau Gododdin.

Hence the idea of Rheged as solely south of Hadrian's Wall, we naturally do not agree with, and will argue that in the sixth century in the land of Pryden or Albion were left numerous Artur references, still found in present day Scotland, which deserve to be considered every bit as much as those Arthurian references south of the Hadrian Wall.

In these early times, the whole of Britain was originally inhabited by mainly British tribes. The criterion was not their geographic location, but whether they spoke a dialect of 'P' Celtic, the British tongue, that decided whether they belonged to the Britons or not. This would include, in the sixth century, many of the northern Caledones and other tribes now called Picts.

They equate Arthur with Arcturus, a star in the constellation of the

Great Bear (the Plough or Big Dipper) and from this association describe Arthur as the Bear of Britain; but if one looks at Welsh literature, the *Triads* and the *Mabinogion*, he is much more associated with the Boar! They then associate Arthur with the Dukes of Warwick, whose standard had the device of the Bear. However Arthur's time was much earlier than these Dukes, while in his time in the north, there was an ancient district known as Warwick (Warewic) around Carlisle. (See Professor N.L. Goodrich's *King Arthur.*)

We would also argue that the Ancient Welsh Genealogies are primarily of the Northern Britons, including many British families north of Hadrian's Wall, in southern Scotland (Pryden), the descendants of Coel Hen Godebog. This fact is not recognised by the authors, leaving the impression that the Genealogies are mainly of the southern Welsh, when they in fact contain only comparatively few southern Welsh families.

The above examples show a few of the differences, in our general approaches to the deductions made, in this well written and intriguing book.

Last but not least, we should mention Meirion Pennar, lecturer at St David's University College, Lampeter in Dyfed, for his up-to-date translations of *Taliesin Poetry* and *The Black Book of Carmarthen.* We hope he will follow up with a translation of the *Canu Aneirin*, which would be a boon to those of us that do not read or speak Welsh with any facility.

CHAPTER 15
CONCLUSIONS

There is a problem in dealing with the Britons of the north, and in particular those north of Hadrian's Wall, as these lands were overrun from the seventh century onwards by the Northumbrians. This resulted in the 'P' Celtic or Brythonic language being much obliterated, between the two Roman walls. The early Saxon tongue became the principal speech, as evinced by the present day Scottish dialects. Only in the north-east of Scotland did the Cumbric tongue survive into the ninth century, when the uniting of the Scots and the Picts brought in the Gaelic as the language of the conquerors. This left the British Kingdom of Strathclyde, and perhaps Galloway and Dumfries, as the last outposts of the Welsh speech in Albion, Pryden or Scotland.

This has meant a great loss of place-names of the northern Britons.

In contrast, Wales, having kept the ancient British or Cumbric language right into this century, naturally identifies from its ancient literature places suggested as localities, recognised mainly within its own boundaries. People forget that other parts of this island were, in times long ago, in the lands of the Britons, with similar British place names, e.g., the river Tweed is the Tywi, the Teviot is the Teifi and there are quite a number of other examples.

However, despite this, there are just sufficient place-names and historical persons that can be identified and located north of Hadrian's Wall, to bring them into a fifth and sixth century history of Dark Age

Britain. This is very much the case with southern Scotland and northern England.

To begin our premise, we start with an attested person in the sixth century named Artur. He was a Christian, brought up under the influence of the most powerful prelate of his time, St Columba of Iona in Dalriada.

There is, however, still much of the old Druid way surviving, so that Artur is exposed to both beliefs and practitioners.

He does not need a nickname or pseudonym to explain his name: *Artur was his name.*

His grandfather and his father, Gabhran and Aidan, both Scottish Kings of Dalriada, had lands in eastern Scotland, around the eastern end of the Antonine Wall and upper reaches of the River Forth near Snawdoun or Stirling, in the ancient land of Mannau Gododdin. These are the lands of the northern mixed Votadinii tribe (the Brythwyr and Combrogi).

The area is sometimes referred to as the Island of the North. It could be the Isle of Avalon, in the tales: our Avolond, which would suggest that the plain of Slammanan, which remembers the old name of Mannan, as does Clackmannan, was very wet in those early days.

They both married women of the Britons, as indeed did Aidan's son Artur, so that on his maternal side, Artur is most certainly of the Britons, and in particular of the Gotadinii or Gododdin, a British tribe, as attested for by the earliest of poems mentioning Artur, 'The Gododdin' by Aneirin, son of Caw of Pryden.

These marriages, because of the British way of matrilineal succession, brought lands in Mannan, in all probability to both generations.

Artur, it would seem, spent a lot of his youth in his mother's lands in Mannau Gododdin, land of the northern Gotadinii. Then in his late teens, he appears to have gone to Urien of Rheged's Hall at Caer Laverock, to have his military training completed, because of Urien's friendly association with his father Aidan.

Aidan, now prospective King of the Scots of Dalriada and a noted military leader, had married into a British family, giving him lands in the east. He was determined to defend his wife's property against the ever present threat of the Angles, Saxons and the northern tribes, as well as others and he left Artur to be his Laird and defender of the eastern end of the Antonine Wall. This located him in the right place to meet the threat from the Northumbrians in their advance to the north.

There is also evidence of Artur having spent some of his youth in the area of Caer Laverock Castle (Fort or Castle of the Lark), from the number of Arthurian references in that part of the country e.g., Loch Arthur, Kirkcudbright and Arthur's Seat, Dumfries etc. Perhaps land rights from his wife Gwenwhyvaur?

Around this time it would have been difficult for Arthur to have acted for Britain, if he was not *of the Britons*. In fact he became a war leader of the Britons defending the eastern end of the Antonine Wall from attack by the Northumbrians and northern tribes.

At this time his father was made King in Dalriada, therefore it is most unlikely that Artur could have been found in Cadbury or Glastonbury: more likely at Glasston, now Glasserton in Dumfries, and never ever at Tintagel Castle in Cornwall!

Artur is a generation after the heroic Men of the North, that is to say, contemporary with their illustrious sons. Therefore his exploits, in the form of a Brythonic bardic verse, is tacked on to those singing the praises to the *Gwyr Y Gogledd.*

His father Aidan got involved in the politics of his British family and found himself involved in the battle of Arftyrydd on the side of Gwendalleau, his wife's cousin, the Chief of the Selgovae tribe still adhering to the old Druid persuasion. The Chief Druid, Bard and advisor to Gwendalleau, was Myrddin, Geoffrey of Monmouth's Merlin. Here Geoffrey of Monmouth mixes up Emrys of Carmarthen, a fifth century Chief Druid, and Myrddin Chief Druid of the Selgovae, as attested for by the participants in the battle of Arftyrydd, in which he is named *c.* 573/4, a sixth century person and so contemporary with Artur and his father Aidan.

Here again Emrys of Carmarthen in Dyfed is mixed up with Myrddin of the North, as is Artur of Dyfed and Artur of Dalriada and Vortipor of Dyfed with Vortigern of the Cornovii in Wroxeter, also Samson of Dyfed and Samson son of Caw in the north. This constant mixing of peoples of the southern Cymry with those of the north deserves thorough investigation, as it does cause some considerable confusion!

Dr Richard Barber suggests that the southern Welsh adopted the exploits of these 'Northern Heroes' into their poetry, so causing this confusion.

The battle of Arftyrydd was lost by Aidan and Gwendalleau to Ryderych Hael and his allies, Peredur and Gwrgi sons of Eliffer Gosgordfawr, and Dinogad of Powys. Both Aidan and Myrddin had to flee the field. Aidan went to Rheged and his relation by marriage, Urien, at his Hall, and we offer Caer Laverock Castle as the location, although there are some who would prefer the Mote of Mark. King Mark or March of Dumnonia, or Damnonia's stronghold, in the romance of Tristan and Iseult, could just as well be placed here as in Cornwall, as this part of Rheged had strong tribal associations with the Cornovii.

'Trystan elopes with Esyllt, wife of March or Mark [ch = k], son of Meirchion i.e., Meirchion Gul of the Selgovae tribe, to the woods of Kelyddon, the Caledonian forest. Later Arthur sends Gwalchmai, son of Loth of Lothian, as a peace maker to Trystan.' (From *A Dictionary of Celtic Mythology* by P. Berresford Ellis.) All suggests the land of Rheged or a southern Scottish locale!

Myrddin fled to Hart Fell in the forest and land of Castle O'Oer, stronghold of Cynfarch O'Oer his kinsman, hoping for his protection. There he became a 'Wild Man of the Woods' hiding frequently in an

Plate 4: Mote of Mark

apple tree. He describes his poor condition in a poem of that name.

From this poem, 'The Apple Tree', we deduce Myrddin's lineage, and present it for general consideration. It does seem to explain why Myrddin was so afraid of Ryderych Hael, and describes their great enmity, leading to the battle of Arftyrydd. After this battle, Urien saw that Aidan was shipped safely back to Dalriada where unexpectedly he became the sixth King, through the intercession of St Columba, making Artur a son of a King.

Aidan, now King, wanted his eldest son Eochaid Find and his wife Creirwy with him in Dalriada. He left his second son Artur to be in charge of his mother's estates of Camelon (note: only one letter different from Camelot) and Avolond. These lands were between the River Avon and the River Almond encompassing the plain of Slammanan, just south of Falkirk in Stirlingshire, the Mannaw or Mannau of the north.

Prior to this it is suggested that Artur, now a young man in his late teens, shortly after the battle of Arftyrydd, went to Rheged to have his education as a warrior completed at the hands of Urien. While there he met and married Gwenwhyvawr, daughter of Gwrtheryn Gwrtheneu, one of Urien's chief advisors, with a very Cornovii tribal name, Brythonic for Vortigern meaning High Chief.

It is offered that Urien's nephew Modred, son of Low or Loth, had his eye also on Gwenwhyvawr, and this was the reason for Modred's resentment of his uncle Artur. Further on in the story, Modred seduced her on Cockleroy Hill, 'the hill on which the King was cuckolded', and they became lovers. Later, as a prize from the battle of the Miathi or Maetae, or the Saxon Camlan battle, against Aidan, where his sons Eochaid Find and Artur were killed, Modred took her to his land in Fife where he made her his 'Queen'. Verbal tradition has her buried in Meigle Churchyard, Perthshire.

Myrddin meanwhile began to recover himself from his wild state in the forest of O'Oer. Descending from Hart Fell via the Bottom Burn and the Water of Milk to its junction with the River Annan, he journeyed along that river to Hoddam Cross, there meeting a kinsman, St Kentigern, son of Owain son of Urien.

Fordun and Jocelyn confirm that Kentigern and Myrddin (Llailoken, or Homo Fastus) met frequently at Hoddam Cross where Kentigern was Priest, and argued on religious matters.

After these sojourns, Myrddin began to lose his fear of Ryderych Hael and started to journey further afield, to where he was educated by his father's kinsmen, at Tinnis Castle, at Drumelzier in Peeblesshire. Here, unfortunately, he was recognised by the shepherds of Meldredus, the local Chief, who was favourable to Ryderych. They attacked and slew him. He was supposedly buried in or near the churchyard of Drumelzier, the site marked by an ancient flowering hawthorn tree, which seeded later generations of such trees on to the plot. It is said one still exists today.

There is a verbal tradition that the wife of Ryderych Hael was having an affair with Meldredus, and that Myrddin, in an attempt to reconcile himself with Ryderych, appraised him of the situation, thus causing Meldredus's enmity: hence his death at Meldredus's retainers' hands. The area to this day is known as Merlindale. There is a prophecy about Myrddin's death, met at Merlindale, but since we are trying to deal in plausible history, it will be left out of the synopsis.

The Northumbrians or Inglis, led by Kentish Jutes and Saxons, meanwhile were spreading northwards, landing in every river mouth that would take their ships, right up into the Beauly Firth in the far north of Scotland.

Two particular happenings then took place. In the middle of the island they attacked and took Low or Loth of the Votadini's southern stronghold of Dinguaroy (in Gaelic Dun Guaire), Ida of Bernicia capturing it and giving it to Aethelfrith Flesaurs, who gave it to his wife Bebba, hence now Bambrough (Bebbanburh) Castle, giving them a base for further expansion into the north. John Marsden in his excellent book *Northanhymbre Saga* suggests that Bebba was a concubine Queen, so causing some embarrassment to the Venerable Bede in his writings.

The Inglis then moved north with Saxon help to their prime target, led by Eocha and Ebissa with the descendants, a landing and settlement on the upper reaches of the River Forth. There, after a time and considerably reinforced, they proceeded to move aggressively to the west with the help of some Caledonian tribes.

Eocha, according to the *Anglo Saxon Chronicles*, had to depart from the North and return to Kent, leaving, it is supposed, Ebissa and his son Ossa Cyllellaur to lead an attack on the farmers of Cadzow at the battle of Goddeu. This brought Artur into the field, fighting his twelve or so battles in and around the Forth-Clyde valley and the Caledonian forest, at sites identified by S. Glennie and W.F. Skene. Artur's victorious campaign brought some eight or so years of peace to the region.

Artur, later, as was his wont, left Camelon to go on a visit to his father in Dalriada, and entrusted his estate to the charge of his wife and his nephew Modred, now 'King' in Fife, little realising the attachment that Gwenwhyvawr and Modred had for each other. They decided to take this opportunity to usurp Artur's Lairdship of his mother's lands, knowing well that there would be a vigorous reaction from Dalriada. They could prepare for the backlash however, evoked the help of the Maetae tribe, and awaited the oncoming battle. It took place somewhere in Strath Carron, close to Camelon.

On the news of the treachery reaching Aidan, he with his elder sons hurriedly left Dalriada and engaged Modred in Strath Carron.

St Columba tells that it was a great victory for Aidan, even though he lost his two eldest sons Eochaid Find and Artur. They, the Dalriadians, called it the battle of the Miathi (Maetae) (Irish Annals: the battle of Mannan in *c.* AD 582.)

In reality it was a defeat, as Aidan quitted the field with some great alacrity, so much so that we do not know whether his sons' bodies were left on the field of battle, buried there or taken back to Dalriada and then to Iona, for consecration and burial by St Columba. A hasty withdrawal was a sure sign of a defeat.

The battle was fought on the River Carron, but southern scribes transcribing verbal traditions used Saxon known names like Camlan for Camelon or Carron, and called it the battle of Camlan, again showing ignorance of places and names of the northern Britons.

Thus ended Artur's life, fighting alongside his father and his brothers, burial place unknown, as stated in the 'Verses of the Graves' in the *Black Book of Carmarthen*. But his earlier exploits against the Inglis had by this time attracted the notice of the Brythonic Bards and he had become a minor hero with a saga of his own. Unfortunately it was not to be sung long in his own Hall in Camelon, as the Northumbrians in *c*. 615/16 split the northern Britons from their cousins in the south, at the battle of Chester, and later over-ran south-east Scotland and Camelon. Luckily the southern Britons, mainly in free Wales, still remembered Artur's saga.

This was rediscovered in the early ninth century by one Nennius, who brought it back into the daylight of time. Nennius has to bear the blame for starting it all!

It is now possible to assert that Artur, son of Aidan, is Artur of military fame and legend, raised by Geoffrey of Monmouth to a fabled 'King', to become the model of such in the Romantic tales of mediaeval times, five or six hundred years after the historical events of his life.

In this discourse we have avoided, as much as possible, trying to make our hypothesis agree with the mediaeval fabled tales. Instead, like Glennie, we have used verbal tradition, where that tradition does not violate reasonable logic, i.e., does not rely on magic or other devices, like the Myrddin prophecy. The exception to this is the discussion of the famous Arthurian sword Caliburn, and how its name is derived, comparing it with another famous sword and showing how they become fabulised, with a detailed discourse on the Round Table.

We used as much as possible of what is accepted as history, with known historical events and, by a process of deduction or, if preferred, imaginative guess work, we tried to join these events together. We explained their relationships to one another, and placed in this setting Artur, Gwenwhyvawr and Myrddin and those associated with them, to give a historical perspective to Artur son of Gabhran, and show, hopefully, that this Artur deserves consideration as the model for Artur of the Romances.

Nowhere have we had to use a lot of imagination, and show that if you select the right target, in the right place, at the right time, you *can* see the wood from the trees.

It is not necessary to get involved in tricky mental gymnastics to try and explain circumstances attributed to fables. If one simply sticks to what is accepted as known history, with minor flights of probability and reasoned guess work, it will give one an acceptable explanation as near to authentic history as one could expect to deduce after 1,500 years.

We have challenged the generally accepted genealogy of Uther Pendragon, showing him to be alive at the beginning of the ninth century and so aware of Nennius' work, his *Historia Brittonum*, enabling Uther to name one of his sons Arthur.

We have produced a genealogy for Myrddin (Merlin) which explains the reason for the great battle of Arftyrydd (Arthuret), and his hatred and fear of Ryderych Hael.

Through matrilineal succession we show how Aidan, son of Gabhran, obtained lands in the east by marrying a daughter of Clydno Eidyn, and suggest Creirwy. This explains how Aidan's sons and in particular Artur were in the east when the Northumbrians arrived on the upper reaches of the River Forth. Artur, defender of the eastern end of the Antonine Wall, attacked and defeated them, in some twelve or so battles.

Matrilineal succession is used to explain how Brude or Bredi, son of Maelgwyn of Gwynedd, was Chief of the northern Picts; how

Cynddylan, son of Llywarch Hen was Chief in Powys, how Morken, Myrddin's father, was Chief in Alcluyd.

Lastly we show that the Tribe of Coel Hen Godebog (old King Cole) was the main progenitor of the Men of the North.

Artur, son of Aidan, son of Gabhran, and descendant of Coel Hen Godebog on his maternal side, fits the bill of sixth-century War leader and minor hero of the northern Cymry, following the example of the Men of the North, the *Gwyr Y Gogledd*, as defender of the eastern end of the Antonine Wall, to warrant special consideration as the historic person of the name: Artur.

We rest our case.

CHRONOLOGY

An error allowance of ± 10 years on any date is acceptable.

c. AD 326   The three **Collas** expelled from Ireland.

c. AD 362   **St Ninian** born.

c. AD 364   Northern tribes revolt against the Romans.

c. AD 397   **St Ninian** sets up '**Candida Cassa**'.

c. AD 410   Romans depart Britain.

c. AD 430   Battle of Coilsfield, **Coel Hen Godebog** killed.

c. AD 515   Battle of Mons Badonicus, victor **Ambrosius Aurelianus**.

c. AD 515   **St Gildas** is born.

c. AD 521   **St Columba** or **Columcille** is born.

c. AD 533   **Aidan Mac Gabhran** is born.

c. AD 550   **Aidan** marries around this time.

c. AD 551   **Eochaid Find**, Aidan's oldest son, born around this time.

c. AD 552   **Gwyar**, daughter of Aidan, born around this time.

c. AD 554   **Artur**, son of Aidan, born around this time.

c. AD 557   **Ida** of Bernicia captures Dinguaroy, later Bambro' Castle, from the Gododdin.

c. AD 558   **Gabhran**, Aidan's father, killed in battle against Picts.

c. AD 561   Battle of Culdrevney. **Columcille** the victor.

c. AD 563   **St Columba** arrives in Kintyre, and is met by his cousin Conail.

c. AD 573   Battle of Arftyrydd, Aidan and Myrddin defeated by **Ryderych Hael**. Artur aged about 18/19 years.

c. AD 574   Battle of Delgu where **Dunchaid** son of Conail, is killed.

c. AD 574 **Conail** son of Comgal dies.

c. AD 574 **Aidan** becomes 6th King of Dalriada.

c. AD 575 Convention of Drumcett.

c. AD 575 **Artur** fights his twelve or so battles.

c. AD 575 Battle of Caer Greu. **Peredur**, son of Ellifer Gosgordfawr, is killed.

c. AD 582 **Artur** killed at the Battle of the Miathi (Maetae Tribe). First battle of Mannan.

c. AD 583 Battle of Slamannan or Mannan. Aidan avenges the death of his sons Eochaid Find and Artur. Second battle of Mannan.

c. AD 584 Aidan fights the Battle of Euboniam, Isle of Man. Third battle of Mannan or Mannand.

c. AD 590 **Urien of Rheged** assassinated at the mouth of the river Low, Northumbria.

c. AD 595 **Owain** son of Urien killed.

c. AD 596 **Brude**, King of Picts, son of Maelgwyn Gwynedd, killed at the battle of Kir Kin or Fortren.

c. AD 597 **St Columba's** death.

c. AD 600 Battle of Catreath, the warriors of Mynyddog annihilated.

c. AD 603 Battle of Degsastan, Aidan Mac Gabhran defeated.

c. AD 608 **Aidan's** death.

c. AD 612 **St Kentigern's** death.

c. AD 643 Death of **Domnal Brec**, last in the Gabhran line of Dalriadic Kings.

c. AD 673 **Venerable Bede** born.

c. AD 691 **St Adomnan** finishes his *Vitae Columba*.

c. AD 704 **St Adomnan's** death.

c. AD 735 **Venerable Bede's** death.

REFERENCES

Page 2   Tacitus, *Annals of Imperial Rome.*
            Miranda Green, *Celtic Goddesses.*

Page 4   Charles Kightly, *Folk Heroes of Britain.*
            Dr Graham Webster, *Rome Against Caractacus.*
            Professor N.L. Goodrich, *King Arthur.*
            St Gildas, *De Excedio.*
            G. Phillips and M. Keatman, *King Arthur – The True Story.*

Page 5   *The Thirteen Treasures of Britain.*

Page 6   *The Thirteen Treasures of Britain.*

Page 8   P. Salway, *Roman Britain.*
            Dr David Breeze, *The Northern Frontiers of Roman Britain.*
            Nennius, *Historia Brittonum.*
            Geoffrey of Monmouth, *History of the Kings of Britain.*

Page 9   P.C. Bartrum, Edit., *Early Welsh Genealogies.*
            Nennius, *Historia Brittonum.*
            Dr Richard Barber, *The Figure of Arthur.*

Page 10   Hywel Dda, *Welsh Law.*
            Nennius, *Historia Brittonum.*

Page 11   A.B. Scott, *The Pictish Nation, its People and its Church.*
            C.J. Tabraham, *Tantallon Castle,* Leaflet.

Page 12   Sir Walter Scott, *Marmion.*
            W.F.H. Nicolaisen, *British Place Names.*

Page 13   T.W. Rolleston, *Celtic Myth and Legend.*

Page 14   Jones and Mattingley, *Atlas of Roman Britain.*
            A.B. Scott, *The Pictish Nation, its People and its Church.*

Page 15   A.B. Scott, *The Pictish Nation, its People and its Church.*
          W.F.H. Nicolaisen, *British Place Names.*
Page 16   Taliesin Poetry.
          Dr John Bannerman, *Studies in the History of Dalriada.*
          A.B. Scott, *The Pictish Nation, its People and its Church.*
          Tacitus, *Annals of Imperial Rome.*
Page 19   Tennyson, *Lady of Shallott.*
          Nennius, *Historia Brittonum.*
          Geoffrey of Monmouth, *History of the Kings of Britain.*
Page 20   Chrétien de Troyes, *Conte de Graal.*
          Lady Charlotte Guest, *The Mabinogion.*
Page 21   Sir Thomas Mallory, *Le Morte d'Arthur.*
Page 22   Nickolai Tolstoy, *The Quest for Merlin.*
          Sir Thomas Mallory, *Le Morte d'Arthur.*
Page 25   Tennyson, *Sir Galahad.*
          Lady Charlotte Guest, *The Mabinogion.*
Page 26   Sir Thomas Mallory, *Le Morte d'Arthur.*
          Lady Charlotte Guest, *The Mabinogion.*
          A.B. Scott, *The Pictish Nation, its People and its Church.*
Page 27   Sir Thomas Mallory, *Le Morte d'Arthur.*
          Lady Charlotte Guest, *The Mabinogion.*
Page 28   Nennius, *Historia Brittonum.*
          Prof. N.L. Goodrich, *King Arthur.*
          Dr Richard Barber, *The Figure of Arthur.*
Page 31   Jones and Mattingley, *Atlas of Roman Britain.*
          St Gildas, *De Excedio.*
          St Adomnan, *Life of Columba.*
Page 32   St Adomnan, *Life of Columba.*
          Sir Thomas Mallory, *Le Morte d'Arthur.*
Page 33   Prof. N.L. Goodrich, *King Arthur.*
          Charles Kightly, *Folk Heroes of Britain.*
Page 34   Jones and Mattingley, *Atlas of Roman Britain.*

Page 36   Jones and Mattingley, *Atlas of Roman Britain.*
Page 37   Peter Solway, *Roman Britain.*
           Charles Kightly, *Folk Heroes of Britain.*
Page 38   A.B. Scott, *The Pictish Nation, its People and its Church.*
           Dr N.J. Higham, *Northumbria* AD *350-1100.*
Page 39   Aneirin, *The Gododdin.*
           Welsh Triads.
           Bonned Gwyr Y Gogledd.
           Dr John Morris, *Age of Arthur.*
Page 40   St Gildas, *De Excedio.*
           Nennius, *Historia Brittonum.*
Page 42   Prof. N.L. Goodrich, *King Arthur.*
           Stuart Glennie, *Arthurian Localities.*
           A.B. Scott, *The Pictish Nation, its People and its Church.*
Page 42   W.F. Skene, *Celtic Scotland.*
           Stuart Glennie, *Arthurian Localities.*
           A.B. Scott, *The Pictish Nation, its People and its Church.*
Page 43   P.C. Bartrum, Edit., *Early Welsh Genealogical Tracts.*
Page 44   E. Shirley, *The Eagles Have Flown.*
           St Gildas, *De Excedio.*
Page 45   St Gildas, *De Excedio.*
           Ven. Bede, *Ecclesiastical History of the English Nation.*
Page 46   St Gildas, *De Excedio.*
           Nennius, *Historia Brittonum.*
Page 47   G. Phillips and M. Keatman, *King Arthur – The True Story.*
           Professor N.L. Goodrich, *King Arthur.*
           Anne Savage, Edit., *Anglo Saxon Chronicles.*
Page 49   W.F. Skene, *Celtic Scotland.*
Page 51   E. Shirley, *The Eagles Have Flown.*
           John Marsden, *Northanhymbre Saga.*
           Ven. Bede, *Ecclesiastical History of the English Nation.*
           N.J. Higham, *The Kingdom of Northumbria* AD *350-1100.*

Page 52   A.B. Scott, *The Pictish Nation, its People and its Church.*
          Ven. Bede, *Ecclesiastical History of the English Nation.*
Page 53   Mocta of Lugbad.
          John Marsden, *The Illustrated Columcille.*
          Ian Finlay, *Columba.*
          A.B. Scott, *The Pictish Nation, its People and its Church.*
Page 54   St Adomnan, *Life of Columba.*
          John Marsden, *Illustrated Columcille.*
          I. Finlay, *Columba.*
Page 55   Ven. Bede, *Ecclesiastical History of the English Nation.*
          Dr John Bannerman, *Studies in the History of Dalriada.*
          P.C. Bartrum, Edit., *Early Welsh Genealogical Tracts.*
Page 56   Dr John Bannerman, *Studies in the History of Dalriada.*
          Yellow Book of Lecan.
          St Adomnan, *Life of Columba.*
Page 58   St Adomnan, *Life of Columba.*
Page 59   W.F. Skene, *Celtic Scotland.*
          Dr John Bannerman, *Studies in the History of Dalriada.*
Page 60   Dr John Bannerman, *Studies in the History of Dalriada.*
Page 61   *Black Book of Carmarthen.*
Page 62   Dr John Bannerman, *Studies in the History of Dalriada.*
          A.B. Scott, *The Pictish Nation, its People and its Church.*
          Dr Richard Barber, *The Figure of Arthur.*
Page 63   Charles Kightly, *Folk Heroes of Britain.*
          A.B. Scott, *The Pictish Nation, its People and its Church.*
          Dr John Bannerman, *Studies in the History of Dalriada.*
Page 64   Dr John Bannerman, *Studies in the History of Dalriada.*
          Cognatio Brychan.
          De Situ Brecheniauc.
          A.B. Scott, *The Pictish Nation, its People and its Church.*
          Elizabeth Sutherland, *In Search of the Picts.*
          W.A. Cummins, *The Age of the Picts.*
          St Adomnan, *Life of Columba.*

Page 66   A.B. Scott, *The Pictish Nation, its People and its Church*.
           Dr John Bannerman, *Studies in the History of Dalriada*.
Page 67   P.C. Bartrum, Edit., *Early Welsh Genealogical Tracts*.
Page 68   Prof. N.L. Goodrich, *King Arthur*.
Page 69   St Adomnan, *Life of Columba*.
Page 70   Nikolai Tolstoy, *The Quest for Merlin*.
           Stuart Glennie, *Arthurian Localities*.
Page 71   Nikolai Tolstoy, *The Quest for Merlin*.
           Stuart Glennie, *Arthurian Localities*.
Page 72   Stuart Glennie, *Arthurian Localities*.
           Nennius, *Historia Brittonum*.
           Prof. N.L. Goodrich, *King Arthur*.
Page 73   Nennius, *Historia Brittonum*.
           Prof. Leslie Alcock, *Arthur's Britain*.
Page 74   Nennius, *Historia Brittonum*.
Page 75   Nennius, *Historia Brittonum*.
Page 76   P. Berrisford Ellis, *Dictionary of Celtic Mythology*.
           Nennius, *Historia Brittonum*.
Page 77   W.F. Skene, *Celtic Scotland*.
           Dr John Bannerman, *Studies in the History of Dalriada*.
           St Adomnan, *Life of Columba*.
Page 79   Tennyson.
           St Adomnan, *Life of Columba*.
Page 81   A.B. Scott, *The Pictish Nation, its People and its Church*.
Page 82   Nennius, *Historia Brittonum*.
           Anna and Graham Ritchie, *Scotland: Archaeology and Early History*.
Page 83   Anna and Graham Ritchie, *Scotland: Archaeology and Early History*.
Page 84   Meirion Pennar, translation of *Bei Lleas Urien* by Taliesin.
           Stuart Glennie, *Arthurian Localities*.
           W.F. Skene, *Celtic Scotland*.
Page 85   A.B. Scott, *The Pictish Nation, its People and its Church*.

Llywarch Hen.

Page 107 Aneirin.

Page 108 Geoffrey of Monmouth, *History of the Kings of Britain.*
Walter of Oxford.
Nennius, *Historia Brittonum.*

Page 109 Geoffrey of Monmouth, *History of the Kings of Britain.*

Page 110 Henry of Huntingdon, *Historia Anglorum.*
William of Newbrugh, *Historia Rerum Anglicarum.*
William of Malmesbury.

Page 111 William of Malmesbury.
Geoffrey of Monmouth, *History of the Kings of Britain.*

Page 112 Geoffrey of Monmouth, *History of the Kings of Britain.*

Page 113 Geoffrey of Monmouth, *History of the Kings of Britain.*

Page 114 Nennius, *Historia Brittonum.*
P.C. Bartrum, Edit., *Early Welsh Genealogical Tracts.*
Lady Charlotte Guest, *The Mabinogion.*

Page 116 P.C. Bartrum, Edit., *Early Welsh Genealogical Tracts.*
Nennius, *Historia Brittonum.*

Page 117 P.C. Bartrum, Edit., *Early Welsh Genealogical Tracts.*
Bonned Gwyr Y Gogledd.

Page 118 *Bonned Gwyr Y Gogledd.*

Page 119 *Bonned Gwyr Y Gogledd.*

Page 120 *Bonned Gwyr Y Gogledd.*

Page 121 *Bonned Gwyr Y Gogledd.*

Page 122 *Bonned Gwyr Y Gogledd.*
P.C. Bartrum, *Early Welsh Genealogical Tracts.*

Page 124 Dr John Bannerman, Plate 5.

Page 125 P.C. Bartrum, *Early Welsh Genealogical Tracts.*

Page 127 Prof. N.L. Goodrich, *King Arthur.*
R.L. Graeme Ritchie, *Chrétien de Troyes and Scotland.*

Page 128 Royal Commission on the Ancient and Historical Monuments of Scotland, Plate 3.
Taliesin.

Professor N.L. Goodrich, *King Arthur.*

P.C. Bartrum, Edit., *Early Welsh Genealogical Tracts.*

Meirion Pennar, Transl., *The Black Book of Carmarthen – Taliesin Poems.*

Page 144 Dr John Bannerman, *Studies in the History of Dalriada.*

Stuart Glennie, *Arthurian Localities.*

Aneirin *The Gododdin.*

Page 145 Stuart Glennie, *Arthurian Localities.*

Aneirin *The Gododdin.*

Geoffrey of Monmouth, *History of the Kings of Britain.*

Page 146 Dr Richard Barber, *The Figure of Arthur.*

Nikolai Tolstoy, *The Quest for Merlin.*

W.F. Skene, *Celtic Scotland.*

P. Berresford Ellis, *Dictionary of Celtic Mythology.*

Stuart Glennie, *Arthurian Localities.*

Page 147 Royal Commission on the Ancient and Historical Monuments of Scotland, Plate 4.

Myrddin, *The Apple Tree.*

Page 148 St Adomnan, *Life of Columba.*

Stuart Glennie, *Arthurian Localities.*

Professor N.L. Goodrich, *King Arthur.*

John of Fordun, *Chronicles of the Scottish Nation.*

Page 149 John of Fordun, *Chronicles of the Scottish Nation.*

Jocelyn, *Life of St Kentigern.*

Stuart Glennie, *Arthurian Localities.*

John Marsden, *Northanhymbre Saga.*

Page 150 Anne Savage, Edit., *The Anglo-Saxon Chronicles.*

W.F. Skene, *Four Ancient Books of Wales.*

St. Adomnan, *Life of Columba.*

Stuart Glennie, *Arthurian Localities.*

Page 151 *Black Book of Carmarthen.*

Nennius, *Historia Brittonum.*

APPENDIX I

THE TRIBES NAMED BY THE ROMANS IN SCOTLAND

(See Map 2 for territories)

The Attacotti

This tribe is something of a mystery. It is mentioned in the fourth century, in *c*. AD 364, as betraying Roman trust, when instead of warning of unrest likely to affect Roman security, they apparently joined a barbarian uprising. This was of such severity that it almost defeated the Roman conquest, and probably brought about the complete abandonment of the Antonine Wall.

They appear to be of Irish connection or extraction, occupying perhaps Kintyre or other west coast sites in Scotland. One is forced back to the explanation of Colla Uais (one of the Three Collas) whose marriage with a 'Queen' of Alba gave a mixed tribe of Britons and Irish in the fourth century. They, like Coel Hen's tribal amalgam, appear to have accepted Roman gold in exchange for keeping the local tribes favourable to Rome and warning the Romans of any likelihood of an attack.

This rebellion was a concerted attack by the Dicalydonaes, the Verturiones, the Attacotti and Scots in Britain, while the Franks and the Saxons assaulted Gaul (see P. Salway's *Roman Britain* pp. 369 and 375). The fact that here the Attacotti and Scots are named separately suggests that the Attacotti are of the Irish Cruithne (Irish Picts) and so it could be argued that they came from the Rhinns of

Galloway, where for some considerable time, Cruithne had been settling.

A.B. Scott suggests that when the Pictish King lists show a joint rule, which is quite frequent, this shows a King of the Southern Picts (i.e., in the Rhinns) and a King of the Northern Picts in Fortren. We know nothing of the Attacotti leaders.

It would appear that the Romans recruited Attacotti as federated troops, which on reflection would give more credence to this tribe, the Attacotti, being the Cruithne of Galloway.

The Boresti

The lost tribe mentioned by Tacitus in his description of Agricola's Scottish campaigns. After defeating the Caledonians under Galgacus at Mons Gropius, the Roman army retired to the comparative safety of the Boresti tribe. It would appear that it got swallowed up into the Maetae alliance.

The Brigantes

One of the largest tribes in all Britain, spreading from southern Scotland (Albion or Pryden), say from Selkirk, over the Hadrian Wall and deep into northern England as far south as York or further.

It is suggested by A.B. Scott that Agricola, in his first Scottish campaign, pushed the northern Brigantes over the River Forth, and that they then formed the nucleus of the Maetae tribe.

This is again a tribal conglomerate which could, as far as the Scottish tribes are concerned, contain some Carvetii, some Selgovae, and possibly some Gotadini, under their tutelage.

Early in the first century lived the famous Chieftainess Cartimandua of the Brigantes, who befriended the Romans and helped them against the uprising of Caractacus, Chief of the Catuvellauni and the Trinovantes. They repaid their debt to her when her husband, whom she had just put aside, tried to oust her from her Chieftaincy, but the Romans came to her rescue, sustaining her in her position.

By the sixth century the Brigantes in Scotland were being absorbed by Rheged, Strathclyde Britons and the Gododdin, as the three principal native states in Southern Scotland.

The Caledonii

A much maligned tribe whose name is often used in a general way to describe all tribes north of the Forth-Clyde line, and more particularly is used as synonymous with the all-embracing name of Picts. This has been taken to mean that they were not a British tribe, but the tribe of this name shown in Ptolemy's map as occupying the massif of the South Grampian range certainly spoke a dialect of 'P' Celtic, the language of the Britons. They are not to be confused with the Dicaledones who appear to be of Irish origin, speaking a dialect of Gaelic, or 'Q' Celtic. Their land was just north of the Forth-Clyde line where the massif of the Ochil Hills starts the Highlands, and is a highland plateau on which centuries earlier Galgacus, High Chief of the Caledones, had harried the first Roman invasion of Scotland.

This land, the line of junction of the highlands with the lowlands, became a mixing area for the highland tribes to intermarry with those of the lowlands, as did the Scottish clans in a later era. This intermarrying gave the name to the peoples around the upper reaches of the River Forth as the land of the Brythwyr or Combrogi, meaning the mixed peoples, Brito-Picts, and covered the area that was known as Mannau Gododdin, the lands of a northern branch of the Gotadinii.

A number of Pictish or Caledonian chiefs or chiefs' sons are named as at the Court of Mynyddog Mwynfawr of Dinas Eidin (Edinburgh), capital city of Mannau Gododdin, around AD 595 to 600. The poem 'The Gododdin' describes them preparing for the disastrous battle of Catreath and so they were contemporary with Artur, who had been killed some eighteen years earlier.

The term Caledones more than likely includes a conglomerate of small Clans, as indeed, it seems, with most of the tribes named by the Romans.

Gartnait, one of the sons of Aidan Mac Gabhran, younger brother to Artur, married a woman of this tribe and so gained the chieftaincy of one of the Caledonian Clans.

The Carvetii

This tribe may have given to Urien, son of Cynfarch O'Oer of the Selgovae, the Chieftaincy of Rheged, also known as the land of the Novantes. One of his wives was Ethni, daughter of Alfrydyl, and since very little is known of this family, it is suspected they were of the Carvetii, whose lands surrounded the head of the Solway Firth. Because of matrilineal succession, the Chieftaincy being hers to bestow, he, a member of the Selgovae, became Chief in Rheged. There is certainly no suggestion of warfare or other form of duress in Urien becoming Chief.

The tribe may well be split, the northern part having protection of the Novantes, whilst the southern side, later separated by the line of Hadrian's Wall, may have had the succour of the Brigantes. Their territory ran from the north side of the Solway Firth, taking in Gretna Green, then to the south, well beyond Carlisle and the Wall, perhaps to Penrith, and to the east to around Brough and its castle, where they met up with the Brigantes.

Not much is known about their leaders, other than Urien and his son Owain, High Chiefs of the Novantes which contained the Carvetii.

The Cornovii or Cornavii

This must be one of the largest and most scattered tribes noted by the Roman geographers. Their name was given to Cornwall; their headquarters and city was at Wroxeter (*Viroconium Cornoviorum*) in Shropshire. Then they spread out to the north, with a scattering in

Cumbria and a branch in Galloway, where one Ninnian or Rinngan, a son of the Chief, was taken as a hostage for the good behaviour of his father and Clan and sent to Rome. After some twelve years in exile he was released and allowed to return home. On his return journey, he sojourned for some time with St Martin of Tours at his monastery, and was so impressed with what he saw that he determined to set up a similar Christian teaching school. On returning to Galloway, he set up Candidda Cassa on the Isle of Whithorn.

It was Ninnian's creation and monastery which did much for the spread of Christianity throughout the land, at the end of the fourth century and into the fifth and sixth. He is the first monk among the Britons named by the Roman historians.

At the extreme north-eastern tip of Scotland, in Caithness, were the Cornavii, a dialectic difference in the pronunciation and spelling, but almost certainly another branch of this widespread tribe. This suggests that the Cornovii were amongst the first wave of British settlers in the colonisation of Britain, landing in the south-west of England and spreading north and north-eastwards, to cover such a wide distribution.

Their most famous Chief was Vortigern, a Saxon name meaning High Chief, the British equivalent being Gwrtheyrn. A descendant of Vortigern at the Hall of Urien of Rheged was Gwrtheyrn Gwrtheneu, obviously of the Cornovii, and father of Gwenwhyvaur who became Artur's wife. The Cornovii are therefore an important tribe in the Artur story.

The Damnonii or Dumnonii

Here again the Roman geographers have named two peoples some five hundred miles apart with the same name. This again suggests that the most northerly, the Damnonii, occupying north Ayrshire and Renfrewshire, with Alclyd as its most northerly point, spreading to the east as far as Cadzow (Hamilton) and Lanark (Llanerch), were an earlier settlement by the tribe from Gaul, who along with the Cornovii had spread northwards. A later wave, found by the Romans in the south-west of England, the Dumnonii, gave their name to modern Devon!

The most famous son of the northern branch was Ryderych Hael, Chief in Alcluyd who, after his hard-won victory at the battle of Arftyrydd, expanded what was Damnonia into Strathclyde, which eventually swallowed up Urien's Rheged and much of southern Scotland. Ryderych's cousin was Myrddin, Bard and Druid advisor to the Selgovae tribe, called by Geoffrey of Monmouth 'Merlin'. The *White Book of Ryderych*, one of the ancient books of Wales, remembers him; some of the writings of Myrddin are contained in this work, as well as in the *Black Book of Carmarthen* and the *Red Book of Hergist*.

This tribe and its Chief, Ryderych Hael, impinge considerably on the story of Artur, in particular on his relationship and enmity with Artur's father Aidan.

The Dicaledones

This tribe or conglomerate was a late discovery by the Romans, who generally called the peoples north of the Forth-Clyde line the Caledones. On finding a tribe who did not appear to speak the normal Brythonic 'P' Celtic tongue of the Caledones, they called them the divided or split Caledones i.e., the Dicaledones, probably speaking Gaelic or 'Q' Celtic.

We have given our belief that they are the mixed descendants of the marriage of Colla Uais and Oilieach, daughter of the Chief of Alba in the fourth century, when the three Collas were driven out of Ireland by Muireadhach Tireach. It is possible that the Attacotti were a sub-division of this tribe. All that is really known about them is that they are Albans, with their land probably around Kintyre, which location always seems to have a relationship with the upper reaches of the River Forth in the east.

The Gotadini, Votadini, Otadini or British Gododdin

These occupied the eastern lands of southern Scotland. The Gotadini had their most northerly fortress at Traprain Law, with their most southerly at Bamburgh Castle (British name Dinguaroy). Their territory to the west was the Eildon Hills, bordering with the Selgovae tribe, and to the east was the North Sea.

Their fortress on the site of Bambro' Castle was, in the sixth century, captured by Ida, King of the Bernicians. It appeared to have been defended bravely by the Warrior Bard Llywarch Hen, one of the heroic Men of the North.

Their most famous leader was Low or Loth, in Welsh Llew or Lleu, Chief of Lothian and Orkney. This latter title, we suspect, was gained through an early marriage with a Chieftainess of Orkney and the Gododdin.

Just north of Bambro' Castle, opposite the Farne Islands, are the rivers of the North and South Low, shown on early maps as the North and South Llew, remembering to this day the Chief who gave his name to Lothian (Lowthian).

His family are certainly connected with Artur, whose sister Gwyar married Loth. Loth's children, Artur's nephews, Modred and Gwalchmai (Gawyane), are in association historically with him, as well as being named in the twelfth century Fables.

The Gotadini were early overrun by the Northumbrians, including northern Mannau Gododdin, taking in Artur's hall of Camelon and estate of Avolond. This meant that his exploits got lost locally, but were remembered in the Halls of the unconquered Britons of Wales, so were preserved in verbal ballad, and found by Nennius among his hotchpotch of ancient verse.

One might as well discuss here the land of Mannau Gododdin, which is a locality and not a tribe (although in the main text we have called the people, the Mannawins), occupied by a mixture of Gotadinii and Northern Caledones, Maetae and Venicones who became known as the Brythwyr or Combrogi (fellow countrymen). The area seemed to have its own Chief, which around AD 600 was one Mynyddog, preparing with allies to take on the might of the Northumbrians to stop their northward advance, and bringing them to battle at a place called Catreath. (We are not wholly convinced that Catterick in Northumberland is Catreath.) This was a disaster for the Britons, who were largely outnumbered but fought bravely, killing seven times their own number, until only one or three and the poet Aneirin escaped. Aneirin, being taken prisoner, had to have his freedom bought.

This heroic poem 'The Gododdin' by Aneirin, son of Caw of Pryden, (as all these tribes are descended from Coel Hen and are related, giving free access to many cross-tribal borders), does give a few names that could be identified in the ancient genealogies, as well as localities that can still probably be identified. In general it is disappointing in the lack of confirmation of the many named persons at the fight.

Considering it was fought within some eighteen or so years after Artur's death, there is only a single mention of him, showing that in his time he was only a minor hero to his British contemporaries, and not the great universal King hero of Geoffrey of Monmouth and later story tellers.

The Lugi

A dark haired race, located in Ross-shire, similar to the Silures of the Severn valley. See Elizabeth Sutherland's *In Search of the Picts*.

The Maetae (Midlanders)

In the first campaigns of the Roman army beyond the Forth-Clyde frontier, the Romans gave only two names to these northern peoples: those on the highland massif were the Caledonii, whilst those on the eastern coastal plain were the Maetae.

As their campaigns progressed they were able to identify more tribal groups, and it would appear that the lands of the Caledonii and the

Matae were shrinking, but this was merely that more tribal names were recognised.

The Clan lands of the Maetae were finalised around the upper reaches of the River Forth, favouring the north side, near present-day Clackmannan, to Stirling, including Bridge of Allan, perhaps as far north as the Pictish capital of Fortren and east along the foothills of the Ochils to around Tilliecoutrie. East of them was the territory of the powerful Venicones, in the sixth century under the Chieftaincy of Modred, son of Loth of Lothian and nephew by marriage to Artur. Modred's overlordship of the Venicones quite possibly included the Maetae, the joint tribes being known as the Verturiones (Men of Fortren). He certainly involved the Maetae in his warfare with Artur.

A.B. Scott suggests that they were the remnants of the northern Brigantes tribe, pushed over the River Forth by Agricola in AD 80, who could certainly be called 'Midlanders' as the Brigantes occupied the centre of greater ancient Britain. The 'B' of Brigantes, replacing the 'P' of Pryden, led to the naming of the Britanic Isles.

They were a troublesome tribe and took part in the great uprising of c. AD 364 against the Romans.

The Dalriadic Scots of Aidan and St Columba's time called the Maetae, the 'Miathi', and describe a battle against them, led by Modred, son of Loth, in which Aidan and his two eldest sons took part. It was said by Columba to be a great Dalriadic victory, despite Aidan losing his two sons, Eocho Find and Artur. The battle was fought in the Strath of Carron near Camelon, called by Southern Saxon scribes ignorant of British names north of Hadrian's Wall, the battle of Camlan, the name of a southern river! This should be the battle of Camelon or even Carron, a northern river.

The Novantes
This tribe is possibly named after the discovery of the Rhins of Galloway, when the Roman fleet in the first century did a

circumnavigation of the British Isles, and was named by the Romans the Novantarum Peninsula. The new peninsula and the peoples of this new discovery were called the Novantes, the new people. They were an amalgam of a number of tribes, principally the Cornovii, the Carvettii, some Selgovae and possibly some Brigantes, while within the Rhins of Galloway were the Irish Cruithne or Irish Picts.

The Novantes covered most of the Clan lands of Rheged and, crossing over the Hadrianic Wall, reached far into Lancashire, and perhaps as far east as Catterick in Northumberland.

In the sixth century lived its most famous Chief, Urien (reigned 570-590) and his eldest son Owain (reigned 590-595), whose son Cyndrwn Garthwys became St Kentigern and later St Mungo of Glasgow.

Urien led an alliance of British tribes against the advancing power of the Northumbrians and drove them off the main land into the sea and on to the Farne Isles. At this point, his second in command, Modred, son of Loth, in a fit of anger and jealousy, had him assassinated, breaking up the alliance, and the Britons drifted back to their homelands, so allowing the Northumbrians to return to the mainland and regroup to take their revenge on the disunited Britons later. According to Llyarch Hen, Urien was killed at Aber Llew (the mouth of the river Low) opposite the Farne Isles.

The Selgovae

A large tribe occupying most of the central lands of Southern Scotland, from the Eildon Hills in the east to the lands and forest of O'Oer in the west, perhaps as far north as Lanark (Llanerch), and to their junctions with the Carvetii and the Brigantes in the south.

In the early sixth century, the ruling family of this powerful Clan, descendants of Meirchion Gul, was the family of his son Cynfarch O'Oer, who did not succeed his father as Chief, owing to matrilineal succession.

The Chieftaincy went either to his widowed mother's new husband (our preferred interpretation) or to the spouse of a sister (unnamed) who married Gwendalleau, son of Cedio of Mannu Gododdin, who became Chief through matrilineal succession, a move that did not appear to meet with the approval of Cynfarch or his progeny.

Cynfarch married a daughter of Brychan of Brechiniog, Nyfain by name, sister to Lluan wife of Gabhran, so that Clan O'Oer was through marriage related to the House of Gabhran. Nyfain gave him his two famous sons, Urien who became Chief in Rheged, and Low or Loth who became Chief of the Gododdin (Gotadinii) and gave his name to the present day Lothians. Cynfarch's brother Elidir Lydanwyn married Nyfain's sister.

The loss of the battle of Arftyrydd by Gwendalleau and Myrddin of the Selgovae, to Ryderych Hael and his allies, broke up this tribe.

There is some evidence that they moved east, and amalgamated with the Gotadinii or Gododdin, under the protection of their Chief Low or Loth who, like his brother Urien, was born of the Selgovae.

The Venicones or Verturiones

They were located on the north side of the River Forth in what is now called the Kingdom of Fife, where some of the best agricultural lands in Scotland are to be found, so one would expect this tribe to be pretty strong to hold on to their land and, indeed, in the great rebellion of AD 364, the Venicones or Verturiones, the Men of Fortren, were one of the principal tribes against the Romans.

Somehow or other, in the sixth century, Modred son of Loth became Chief of the Venicones/Verturiones, probably through an early marriage, and, invoking the help of the Maetae, usurped Artur's lairdship of his mother's estate at Camelon, bringing Artur, led by his father Aidan, to battle at Strath Carron. This was described by the Dalriadic Scots as the battle of the Miathi, at which Artur and his elder brother were killed. As a prize for his defeat of Artur and his father

Aidan, Modred took Artur's wife Gwenwhyvaur back to Fife and there made her his 'Queen'.

These are the tribes most involved in the Artur story.

Not much is known about the tribes further north, other than their suggested locations, as follows: the Epidii in south Kintyre (the horse people); the Creones around Appin; the Scetis in Skye; in the east, in the Grampians the Vacomagi; further east around Aberdeen the Taezali. North of the Great Glen in the west, the Carnocacae and the Carenii; in the east the Decantae (this could be a northern dialectic name of the southern Decangi or Decealngi); then the Lugi in Ross-shire and in the extreme north the Smertae; lastly the Cornavii (Cornovii) in Caithness.

In the outer Hebrides, in Lewis and Harris, was the domain of the Dumna.

APPENDIX II

FEMALES LISTED IN THE

EARLY WELSH GENEALOGIES

(f) = daughter

Adies (f) Iarll Claer, wife of Cadwalader son of Gruffud.

Adwen (f) Brychan.

Adwent (f) Eilffer, wife of Enflew.

Afandreg (f) Gwair, wife of Iago son of Idwal.

Afandreg (Tandreg) Ddu (f) Cynan Garwyn, wife of Cadfan son of Iago.

Afandreg (f) Gwrgi, wife of Owain Gwynedd.

Afrella wife of Umbraphel.

Agenst (f) Gruffud.

Ananan Lleian (f) Helig.

Anawfedd (f) Ensic, wife of Budic son of Cybrdan.

Anedd (f) Gwrgi, wife of Owain Gwynedd.

Angharad (f) Brochwell, wife of Caradog Hardd son of Gwrydr.

Angharad (f) Cadwaladr.

Angharad (f) Genillin, wife of Cynan son of Owain Gwynedd.

Angharad (f) Hwfa, wife of Cynwrig son of Iorwerth.

Angharad (f) Llawr and Lleucu, wife of Cadwgon son of Elystan Glodrydd.

Angharad (f) Llyeldyn, wife of Owain son of Hywel Dda.

Ahgharad (f) Maredudd, wife of (1) Llywelyn son of Seisyll, (2) Cynfyn son of Gwerystan.

Angharad (f) Meurig, wife of Rhodri Mawr.

Angharad (f) Owain son of Edwin, wife of Gruffud, son of Cynan.

Angharad (f) Owain Gwynedd, son of Gruffud, wife of Gruffud Maelor.

Angharad (f) Peredur, wife of Owain Gwynedd.

Anna wife or mother to Beli Mawr.

Anna (f) Uther Pendragon, wife of Cynyr of Caer Gawch.

Archfedd (f) Arthur, wife of Llawfrodedd Farchog.

Arddun Benasgell (f) Pabo, wife of Brochwell Ysgithrog.

Banhadlwedd (f) Banadl.

Beilo (f) Brychan.

Belyau (f) Brychan.

Bethan (f) Brychan.

Blodeuwedd (f) Math and Arianrhod.

Brawstudd (f) Gloud, wife of Arthfael son of Gwriad.

Cain Breit or **Ceinwen** (f) Brychan.

Cainel (Irish **Caemelli**) wife of Bwrrwinen.

Cairinne (f) Brychan.

Ceindeg (f) Llwyarch Hen.

Ceindrech (f) Brychan.

Ceindrech (f) Rheiden, wife of Macsen Weldig.

Ceindrech (f) Rhiwallon, wife of Gwlyddien.

Ceinfron (f) Lwyarch Hen.

Ceinfryd (f) Cyndrwyn.

Ceinfryd (f) Ednywain Bendew, wife of Cynddelw son of Cwnws.

Ceinfryd (f) Rhidri Mawr, (1) wife of Gruffud son of Llywelyn son of Seisyll. (2) wife of Trahaeddarn son of Maelog.

Ceingair (f) Brychan, wife of Gwynllyw.

Ceingair (f) Maredudd, wife of Gwriad son of Brochwel.

Ceinwen (f) Brychan, see Cain Breit.

Ceinwen Fechan (f) Ieuan Degan, wife of Endos or Dos son of Deigr.

Celeinion (f) Hywel, wife of Hwfa son of Llywarch Goch.

Celeinion or **Celenion** (f) Tudwal son of Anarawd, wife of Sandde son of Alcwn.

Cenaf (f) Tewdwr Mawr.

Cenedlon (f) Briafael Frydig.

Cenedlon (f) Brychan, see Cynheiddon.

Cerddych (f) Brychan.

Clydai (f) Brychan.

Creirbia (f) Fracan.

Creirwy (f) Clydno Eidyn – see Euronwy.

Cristin (or **Efa**) (f) Bledrus, wife of Maredudd son of Bleddyn.

Cristin (f) Gronw, wife of Owain Gwynedd.

Cwyllog (f) Caw.

Cynheiddon (f) Brychan.

Danhadlwen (f) Cynyr of Caer Gawch, wife of Dirdan.

Deichter (f) Muiredach Muinderg, wife of Sawyl Benisel.

Denw or **Denyw** (f) Lleuddun Luyddog, mother of Cynderyn Garthwys.

Derwel sister of Amon and mother of Machudd.

Dina (f) wife of Brychan.

Dolgar (f) Gildas.

Don (f) Mathonwy.

Drynwin (f) Brychan.

Dwyn (f) Brychan.

Dwywai (f) Lleenog, wife of Dunod Fwr.

Dwywei (f) Cunedda Foel or (f) Tegaid Foel.

Dyddgu (f) Madog, wife of Rhotbert son of Llywarch.

Dyddgu (f) Maredudd, wife of Cadwalader, son of Gruffudd.

Dyfwn (f) Glywys, wife of Meurig son of Caradog.

Eberth (f) Iaen, see Eleirch.

Edwen (f) Brychan.

Efa (f) Bledrus, see Cristin (f) Bledrus.

Efeilian (f) Cadfan, wife of Gwydr Drwm.

Efrddyl (f) Cynfarch O'Oer, wife of Eliffer Gosgodfawr.

Efrddyl (f) Pebio Glafrog.

Eigr (f) Amlawdd Weldig, wife of Gwrlais and Uther Pendragon.

Eiliwedd (f) Brychan.

Eleirch (Eberth) (f) Iaen, wife of Arthur?

Elen Luyddog (Helen Luitdauc) (f) Coel, wife of Constantius Chlorus.

Elen (f) Eudaf Hen, wife of Macsen Weldig.

Elen (f) Llywarch, wife of Hywel Dda.

Elen (f) Tewdwr Mawr, wife of Bleddyn son of Maenyrch.

Ellylw (f) Cydifor, wife of Cadwgon.

Ellylw (f) Elidir, wife of Llywelyn son of Cadwgon.

Elufed (f) Peredur, wife of Tudwal Tutclyd.

Enghenedl (f) Elise.

Enynny (Enhinti) (f) Cynfarch, wife of Tewdrig and mother of Meurig.

Erdudfyl (f) Cynfarch O'Oer, see Efrddyl.

Estedich (f) Efryddl.

Esyllt (Etthil) (f) Cynan Dindaethwy, wife or mother of Merfyn Frych.

Ethni Wyddeles wife of Rhicwlff son of Tudwal Tutclyd.

Ethni Wyddeles (f) Mathylwch, wife of Gwynnog son of Coleddog.

Ethni (f) Alfryd, wife of Gwrfyw son of Pasgen.

Eurbrawst wife of Brychan.

Eurdre (f) Trahaearn, wife of Y Blaidd Goeg.

Euedrich (f) Diwrig, wife of Trahaearn son of Maelog Dda.

Eurgain (f) Maelgwn Gwynedd, wife of Elidir Mwynfawr.

Euronwy (f) Clydno Eidyn, wife of Gwaith Hengaer, or Urien of Rheged.

Ffefur or **Ffener** (f) Cyndrwyn, see Ffreuer.

Ffranges 'French woman', (f) Pictot, wife of Cadwgon son of Bleddyn.

Ffynnod Weddeles wife of Owain Gwynedd.

Generys (f) Cynfyn Hirdref.

Generys (f) Rhys Sais, wife of Ednywain son of Ithel.

Genilles (f) Gwrgeneu, wife of Gwalchmai son of Meilir.

Genilles (f) Hoedlyw, wife of Gronw son of Owain.

Gloyw (f) Brychan, error for Goleu.

Goleu (f) Brychan.

Gratian (f) Macsen Weldig, wife of Tudwal son of Morfawr.

Greddyf (f) Cwnws Ddu.

Gwallwen (f) Afalach, wife of Maelgwn Gwynedd.

Gwawl (f) Ceredig.

Gwawl (f) Coel, wife or mother to Cunedda.

Gwawr (f) Brychan, wife of Elidir Lydanwyn.

Gwawr (f) Ceredig, wife of Glywys.

Gwawrddydd (f) Brychan, error for Cerddych.

Gwen (f) Brychan.

Gwen (f) Ceredig, wife of Pedrwn son of Emyr Llydaw.

Gwen (f) Cunnedda Weldig, wife of Amlawd Weldig.

Gwen (f) Cynyr of Caer Gawch, wife of Selyf (wife of Geraint).

Gwen (f) Tewdwr Mawr see Tengo.

Gwen Teitbron (f) Emyr Llydaw, wife of Cadfan.

Gwenabwy (f) Caw, wife of Llwydeu son of Nwython (Pictish).

Gwenasedd (f) Rhain of Rhieinwg, wife of Sawyl Benisel.

Gwenddydd (f) Cyndrwyn.

Gwenddydd (f) Brychan.

Gwenfaen (f) Paul Hen.

Gwenfrewy (f) Brychan.

Gwenfrewy (f) Tyfid.

Gwenhaf (f) Llifonwy, wife of Ensic.

Gwenhwyfach (f) Orgfan Gwar, wife of Modred, son of Caindraf.

Gwenllian (f) Cynan, wife of Cadwgon son of Llywarch.

Gwenllian (f) Ednyfed, wife of Rhirid Flaidd.

Gwenllian (f) Ednywain, wife of Owain Gwynedd.

Gwenllian (f) Gruffudd, son of Cynan, wife of Cadwgon, son of Bleddyn.

Gwenllian (f) Gruffudd, son of Cynan, wife of Gruffudd son of Rhys.

Gwenllian (f) Hywel, wife of Iorwerth son of Llywarch.

Gwenllian (f) Maddog, wife of Rhys Mwynfawr son of Gruffudd.

Gwenllian (f) Owain Gwynedd, wife of Owain Cyfeilog.

Gwenllian (f) Rhys, mother of Einudd.

Gwenlo (f) Bugi (Insi), wife of Tyfid.

Gwennan (f) Brychan.

Gwenrhiw (f) Brychan.

Gwenwen (Gwenneuuen) (f) Iderneth.

Gweurfyl (f) Gwrgeneu, wife of (1) Cadwaladr son of Gruffudd, (2) Gruffud son of Maredudd.

Gweurfyl (f) Owain Cyfeiliog, wife of Hywel son of Iorweth.

Gwladus wife of Brychan.

Gwladus (f) Aidus, wife of Ednyfed son of Cynwrig.

Gwladus (f) Brychan, wife of Gwynllyw son of Glywys.

Gwladus (f) Cyndrwyn.

Gwladus (f) Gruffudd, wife of Caradog son of Iestyn.

Gwladus (f) Llywarch Hen, son of Elidir Lydanwyn.

Gwladus (f) Llyarch son of Trahaearn, wife of Owain Gwynedd.

Gwladus (f) Rhiwallon, wife of Rhys son of Tewdwr.

Gwladus (f) Ryderych Hael (wrongly wife of Brwydr Ddiriaid).

Gwledyr (f) Clydwyn.

Gwledyr (f) Cyndrwyn.

Gwledyr (f) Seisyll, wife of Gwrgeneu son of Ednywain.

Haer or **Hyar** (f) Cillin, wife of Cynfyn son of Y Blaidd Rhud.

Haer (f) Y Blaidd Rhud, wife of Cynfyn Hindref.

Hawstyl (f) Brychan, error for Tudwystl.

Heled (f) Cyndrwyn.

Hunydd (f) Bran, wife of Gruffudd son of Carwed.

Hunydd (f) Brychan, wife of Tudwal Befr.

Hunydd (f) Einudd, wife of Maredudd son of Bleddyn.

Illud (f) Brychan.

Ina (f) Ceredig.

Iuliana (f) Brychan.

Iwerydd (Ywerit) mother of Bran.

Iwerydd (f) Cynddelig Bennog, wife of Iarddur son of Môr.

Iwerydd (f) Cynfyn, wife of Edwin son of Gronw.

Llechid (f) Ithel Hael.

Lleian (f) Brtchan, error for Lluan.

Llenwedd (or **Lleunedd**) (f) Egri.

Lleucu (f) Enflew and Adwent, wife of Morgan son of Owain.

Lleucu (f) Gwrgeneu, wife of Rhiwallon son of Gwrydr.

Lleucu (f) Maredudd, wife of Llawr.

Lluan (f) **Brychan**, wife of Gafran (Gabhran).

Llud (f) Brychan, error for Ilud.

Llychwy of Llanbeulan, wife of Gruffudd son of Cynan.

Madrun (f) (a) Gwerthefyr Fendigaid, wife of Ynyr Gwent.

      (b) Gwrtheyrn Fendigaid.

Magna sister to Dewi, mother of Setna.

Mailcorcre (Maelgreg) (f) Dunlag, wife of Afloed (Olaf Arnaid), son
of Sutrig.

Marared (Margaret, Mared or **Marfred)** (f) Gruffudd, wife of Ieuaf
son of Owain.

Marared (f) Madog, wife of Iorwerth son of Owain Gwynedd.

Marchell (f) Awstl Gloff.

Marchell (f) Brychan, wife of Gwrin Farfdrwch.

Marchell (f) Tewdrig, wife of Anlach.

Margred (f) wife of Llyr Marini.

Mechyll (f) Brychan, error for Marchell.

Meddfyl (or **Medwyl**) (f) Cyndrwyn.

Meddwid (Meddvyth) (f) Idloes.

Meddyf (f) Maeldaf.

Medlan (f) Cyndrwyn.

Medlan Benllydan (f) Neiniad, wife of Gollwyn son of Tango.

Medwyl (f) Cyndrwyn see Meddfyl.

Meiriones (f) Feiriones, wife of Owain Gwynedd.

Meisir (f) Cyndrwyn.

Melangell (f) Rhicwlff (or Cyfwlch).

Meleri (f) Brychan, wife of Ceredig son of Cunnedda Weldig.

Menfre (f) Brychan, (Menefrida).

Merewenne (f) Brychan (Morewenna).

Morfudd (f) Elfan, wife of Owain Gwynedd.

Morfudd (f) Ednywain Bendew see Morwyl, wife of Owain son of Edwin.

Morfudd (f) Merwydd Hir, wife of Owain Gwenedd.

Morfudd (Morud) (f) Urien of Rheged.

Nefydd (f) Brychan, error for Hunydd.

Nefyn (f) Brychan, error for Nyfain.

Nest (f) Cadell, wife or mother of Merfyn Frych.

Nest (f) Cynfyn, wife of Ithel of the Bryn.

Nest (f) Gruffudd, wife of Ifor Bach.

Nest (f) Rhodri Mawr, mother of Morgan son of Owain.

Non (**Nonnita**) (f) Cynyr of Caer Gawch, wife of Sant, see Nonnwyn Greg.

Nonnwyn (f) Ynyr Freichgoch, see Non.

Nwnengreg (f) wife of Meurig son of Idno.

Nyfain (f) Brychain, wife of Cynfarch O'Oer son of Meirchion Gul.

Peithen (f) Caw.

Peren (f) Greidal, wife of Cynwyd Cynwydion.

Perisgri wife of Brychan.

Perweur (f) Crydr Fychan, wife of Cadfael son of Aeddan.

Perweur (f) Cynfyn Hindref, wife of Diwrig son of Bledrus.

Perweur (f) Rhotbert, wife of Sandde son of Iarddur.

Perweur (f) Rhun Ryfeddfawr, wife of Rhun son of Maelgwyn.

Prawst wife of Brychan (**Eurbrast, Rhybrawst, Proistri, Perisgri**).

Prawst (f) Cynddelw, wife of Bledrus son of Gruffudd.

Prawst (f) Elise, wife of Seisyll.

Prawst (f) Tidlet or Tithlym, wife of Einion Yrth.

Proistri (**Proestri, Perisgri**), wife of Brychan.

Rhael (**Rhuel**), (f) Gronw, wife of Llywarch son of Bran.

Rhael (**Rhuel**), (f) Gruffudd, wife of Llywarch son of Bleddyn.

Rhagaw (f) Llyr see Rhegau.

Rhagaw (f) Llywarch Hen.

Rhanillt (**Ragnell**) (f) Afloed, wife of Cynan son of Iago.

Rhanillt (f) Gruffudd, wife of Madog son of Iderneth.

Rhea Silva (f) Numa Pampilius, wife of Fetebir.

Rhegau (**Regau, Rhagaw**) (f) Llyr, wife of Henwyn.

Rhiceneth (**Ricceneth**), wife of Morgan or Morcant son of Artrwys.

Rhieingar or **Rhiengar** (f) Brychan.

Rhieinwyldd (**Rieingulid**) (f) Amlawdd Weldig, wife of Bicanus.

Rhiell (**Rhuell**) (f) Llywarch Hen.

Rhybrawst wife of Brychan.

Sanan (f) Cynfyn Hindref, wife of Gwgon of Llyn.

Sanan (f) Cyngen, wife of Maelgwyn Gwynedd.

Sanan (f) Dinwal or Dyfnwal.

Sanan (f) Elise, wife of Nowy, King of Powys.

Sanffraid (f) Dwthach (St Bride, Brigit).

Saradwen wife of Gwyddno Garanhir.

Severa (**Sevira**) (f) Macsen Weldig.

Stradweul (f) Gadeon see Ystradwel.

Susanna (f) Gruffudd, son of Madog son of Maredudd.

Sylwein (f) Geraint.

Tandreg (**Afandreg**) **Ddu** (f) Cynan Garwyn, wife of Cadfan son of Iago.

Tandreg (f) Rhys, wife of Meilir son of Mabon.

Tanglwyst (f) Brychon.

Tangwre or **Tegiwg** (f) Gwyn, wife of Seisyl son of Gwrgi.

Tangwystl (f) Brychan.

Tangwystl (f) Cadwallon, wife of Cadwaladr son of Gruffudd.

Tangwystl (**Tancoysl**) (f) Owain, wife of Bleddig or Bledri.

Tedda (f) Brychan.

Tegau Eurfron, wife of Caraddog Freichfras.

Tegeingl (**Tecgygl**) (f) Cunedda Weldig.

Tegfedd (f) Tegid Foel, wife of Cedig or Ceredig.

Tegid (f) Cunedda Weldig.

Tegiwg (f) Gwyn see Tangwre.

Tegiwg (f) Ynyr Gwent.

Tegno (**Tenaf**, **Cenaf**) (f) Tewdwr Mawr, wife of Alltu Redegog.

Tenoi (**Tonwy**) (f) Lewdun Luyddog, wife of Dingad son of Nudd Hael.

Thewer (f) Brydw, wife of Casanauth Weldig.

Tonwen (f) Cynyr of Caer Gawch.

Tubrawst (**Dubrawst**), wife of Argud (Elgud), son of Cadfarch.

Tudfyl (f) Brychan.

Tuglid (f) Brychan, wife of Cyngen Glodrydd.

Tudwen (f) Brychan.

Tudwystl (f) Brychan.

Tybie (f) Brychan.

Tydiau (f) Brychan.

Tywanwedd (**Dwyanwedd**, **Dywanwedd**) (f) Amlawd Weldig, wife of: (1) Awstl Gloff. (2) Tudfwlch Gorneu.

Wencu son or daughter of Brychan.

Wenheden son or daughter of Brychan.

Wenna (f) Brychan.

Wensent son or daughter of Brychan.

Wynup (**Wennepa**) (f) Brychan.

Yneigr (f) Tudfwlch, wife of Rhiwallon son of Gwrydr.

Ynghrad see **Anghrad**.

Ysbaenes 'Spanish Woman', wife of Brychan.

Yslani or **Slani** (f) Brien, wife of Sutrig son of Afloed.

Ystradwel or **Stradweul** (f) Gadeon son of Cynan, wife of Coel Hen Godebog.

APPENDIX *III*

CONTEMPORARIES OF ARTUR

Bleiddud son of Asser, son of Bleidudd.

Brwydr Ddiriaid or **Bedwyr** son of Gwyddien Astrus, son of Deigr.

Caradog son of Lles Llawddeog, son of Cedio.

Cenav son of Gwyddien Astrus, son of Deigr.

Cyfwlch or **Rhicwlff** son of Tudwal Tutclyd, son of Clynog or Ceredig.

Cynfelyn Drwsgl son of Cynwyd Cynwydion, son of Cenfelyn.

Cynfyn Glaer son of Tudwal Tutclyd, son of Clynog or Ceredig.

Dwg and the many other sons of Llywarch Hen, son of Elidir Lydanwyn.

Elfin son of Urien, son of Cynfarch O'Oer.

Elidir Mwynfawr son of Gwrwst Briodor, son of Gwydol.

Gwalchmai son of Low or Loth, son of Cynfarch O'Oer.

Gwynnog Farfsych son of Lles Llawddeog, son of Cedio.

Ieuaf son of Gwyddien Astrus, son of Deigr.

Kynlluc (St) son of Cynr Genhir, son of Cenfelyn.

Kynon or **Cynon** son of Clydno Eidyn, son of Cenfelyn.

Madog one of the many sons of Llywarch Hen, son of Elidir Lydanwyn.

Modred or **Medraut** son of Low or Loth, son of Cynfarch O'Oer.

Mordaf son of Serwan, son of Clynog or Ceredig.

Morgan Mwynfawr son of Tudwal Tutclyd, son of Clynog or Ceredig.

Owain son of Urien, son of Cynfarch O'Oer.

Pasgen son of Urien, son of Cynfarch O'Oer.

Rhiwallon son of Urien, son of Cynfach O'Oer.

Rhun or **Run** (Priest in Northumbrian Church) son of Urien, son of Cynfarch O'Oer.

Rhydderch Hael son of Tudwal Tutclyd, son of Clynog or Ceredig.

Sandref B.A. (**Bryd Angel**) and others of the family of Llywarch Hen, son of Elidir Lydanwyn.

Yspys son of Cadrod Calchyndd, son of Cenfelyn.

These are all six generations from Coel Hen Godebog, and most, if not all, would be known to Artur son of Aidan.

The large family of Llywarch Hen, of which only three names are represented above, are all contemporaries of our Artur; similarly with the sons of Caw of Pryden. See Appendix IV.

Artur is closely related to many of the above, through his maternal descent and British wife.

APPENDIX IV
CHILDREN OF LLYWARCH HEN AND CAW OF PRYDEN

Llywarch Hen

1. Gwen
2. Pill
3. Llawr
4. Mechydd
5. Maen
6. Dwywg
7. Nefydd
8. Sanddef
9. Selyf
10. Dilig
11. Lliuer
12. Deigr
13. Rhut
14. Madawg
15. Medel
16. Heilin
17. Gwell
18. Sawyl
19. Llorien
20. Keny
21. Llynghedwy
22. Kynllug
23. Llewenydd
24. Gorwynion
25. *Rheil*
26. Kenev
27. Kynddylan
28. Talan
29. Kynvarch
30. Rreged
31. Gredwal
32. Gwawr

Caw of Pryden of Dwrkelyn

1. Dirmic
2. Kilid
3. Vstig
4. Echymwg
5. Cof
6. Aneirin
7. Gwydrein
8. Samson
9. Bangar
10. Kelyn
11. Hueil
12. Gildas
13. Aeddan
14. Gwallag
15. Eirgrawn
16. Dyfnwe
17. Gwrddelw
18. *Anev*
19. *Kowyllawg*
20. *Peithien*
21. *Gwenawy*

Note: Names in italics are probably daughters.

BIBLIOGRAPHY

Ailred, *The Life of St. Ninian* (Llanerch 1989).

Anderson, A.O. *Early Sources of Scottish History* 2 Vols. Facsimile Edition (Paul Watkins, Stamford 1994).

Ashe, Geofrey *Mythology of the British Isles* (Guild Publishing 1990) and (Ed) *The Quest for Arthur's Britain* (Paladin Books 1971).

Bannerman, Dr John, *Studies in the History of Dalriada* (Scottish Academic Press 1972).

Barber, Chris, *More Mysterious Wales* (David and Charles 1986).

Barber, Dr Richard, *The Figure of Arthur*, *King Arthur* and *The Arthurian Legends* (Brewer & Boydell Press).

Bartrum, P.C., Editor, *Early Welsh Genealogical Tracts* (Cardiff 1966).

Bede, Venerable, *A History of the English Church and People* (Penguin 1955).

Breeze, David J., *Northern Frontiers of Roman Britain* (Batsford 1982).

Bryce, Derek, *Arthur and the Britons in Wales and Scotland*: Edited edition of W.F. Skene's work (Llanerch Enterprises 1988).

Byrne, Professor Francis J., *Irish Kings and High Kings* (B.T. Batsford, London 1973).

Chadwick, Nora, *The Celts* (Pelican Books 1971 to 1978).

Cherici, Peter, *Celtic Sexuality* (Gerald Duckworth, London 1995).

Clarke, Stevens Reynolds, *Vestigia Anglicana* (P.G. Underwood 1826).

Coghlan, Ronan, *The Encyclopaedia of Arthurian Legend* (Element Books Ltd., 1991).

Donaldson, Gordon, *Scottish Historical Documents* (Scottish Academic Press, Edinburgh 1974).

Dyer, James, *Ancient Britain* (Guild Publishing 1990).

Ellis, Peter Beresford, *Dictionary of Celtic Mythology* (Constable, London 1992).

Eyre-Todd, George, *The Story of Glasgow* (Blackie and Son, Glasgow, 1911).

Finlay, Ian, *Columba* (W. & R. Chambers, Edinburgh, 1991).

Ford, P.K., *The Poetry of Llywarch Hen* (University of California Press, 1974).

Fordun, John of, *Chronicles of the Scottish Nation* 2 Vols. (Llanerch Enterprises).

Forrest, H.E., *The Old Houses of Shrewsbury* (Wilding and Son, Shrewsbury, 1935).

Gerber, Pat, *The Search for the Stone of Destiny* (Canongate 1992).

Glennie, Stuart, *Arthurian Localities.*

Goodrich, Professor N.L., *King Arthur* (Franklin Watts 1989).

Grant, I.F., *Lordship of the Isles* (Murray Press 1935).

Green, Miranda, *Celtic Goddesses* (British Museum Press 1995).

Gueste, Lady Charlotte, *The Mabinogion*, Facsimile (John Jones, Cardiff 1977).

Higham, N.J., *The Kingdom of Northumbria AD 350 to AD 1100* (Alan Sutton 1993).

Higham, N. and Jones B., *The Carvetii* (Allan Sutton Publishing 1985).

Jackson, Antony, *The Pictish Trail* (The Orkney Press 1989).

Jackson, Kenneth, *The Gododdin* (Edinburgh University Press 1968).

Jacobs, Joseph, Editor, *Celtic Fairy Tales* (Studio Editions Ltd. 1990).

Jocelyn, *The Life of St Kentigern* (Llanerch 1989).

Johnson, Stephen, *Later Roman Britain* (Routledge and Kegan Paul 1980).

Johnston J.B., *Place Names of Scotland* (David Douglas, Edinburgh 1903).

Johnstone, Fiona, *Place Names* (Spurbooks 1982).

Kightly, Charles, *Folk Heroes of Britain* (Thames & Hudson, London, 1982).

Legg, Rodney, *Romans in Britain* (Heinemann, London 1983).

Lindsay, Maurice, *The Lowlands of Scotland, Glasgow and the North* and *The Lowlands of Scotland, Edinburgh and the South* (Robert Hale, London 1977).

Livingstone, Helen, *In the Footsteps of Caesar: Walking Roman Roads in Britain* (Book Club Associates 1995).

Mac Sween and Sharp, *Prehistoric Scotland* (B.T. Batsford 1989).

MacLauchlan, Rev. Thomas, *The Scottish Highlands, Highland Clans, and Highland Regiments* (A. Fullarton, Edinburgh and London 18??).

Malory, Sir Thomas, *Le Morte d'Arthur* (Penguin 1969 and McMillan, New York 1900).

Marsden, John, *Northanhymbre Saga* (Kyle Cathie, London 1992) and *The Illustrated Columcille* (Macmillan, London 1991).

Matthews, John, *An Arthurian Reader.*

Matthews, John and Caitlin, *The Aquarian Guide to British and Irish Mythology.*

Mitchel and Robinson, *A Guide to Old English* (Guild Publishing 1968).

Monmouth, Geoffrey of, *History of the Kings of Britain* (Penguin 1966).

Morris, John, *The Age of Arthur* (George Weidenfield & Nicolson, London 1973), *Londonium* (Book Club Associates 1982) and *British History and the Welsh Annals* (Philmore 1980).

Muir, Richard, *History from the Air* (Michael Joseph, London 1983).

Musgrone, Frank, *The North of England: a History* (Basil Blackwell Ltd. 1990).

Myres, J.N.L., *The English Settlements* (Clarendon Press 1986).

Nennius, *Historia Brittonum.*

Ordnance Survey, 1:625,000 Map of Ancient Britain, The Antonine Wall and Hadrian's Wall.

Pennar, Meirion, Translations of *Taliesin Poems, Black Book of Carmarthen* (Llanerch Enterprises 1988).

Pevsner, Nikolas, *The Buildings of England – Shrewsbury.*

Piehler, H.A., *Scotland, a practical and historical guide* (J.M. Dent, London 1963).

Rivet and Smith, *The Place Names of Roman Britain* (B.T. Batsford 1979).

Ritchie, Drs Anna and Graham, *Scotland: Its Archaeology and Early History* (Edinburgh University Press 1991).

Ritchie, R.L. Graeme, *Chrétien de Troyes.*

Rolleston, T.W., *Celtic Myths and Legends* (Avenel Books, New York, 1986).

Room, Adrian, *British Place Names* (Longman 1985).

Ross, Stewart, *Ancient Scotland* (Lochar Publishing, Moffat, 1991).

Salway, Peter, *Roman Britain* (Oxford University Press 1981).

Savage, Anne, *The Anglo Saxon Chronicles*, Translated and Collated (Phoebe Phillips 1984).

Speed, John, *The Counties of Britain*, a Tudor Atlas.

Stewart, R.L., (Ed), *The Book of Merlin* (Blandford Press 1987).

Stone, Jeffrey, *Illustrated Maps of Scotland*, Blaeu's Atlas, 17th Century (Studio Editions, London 1991).

Sutherland, Elizabeth, *In Search of the Picts* (Constable, London 1994).

Tacitus, *Annals of Imperial Rome* (BCA and Penguin Books 1990).

Tolstoy, Nicolas, *The Quest for Merlin* (Hamish Hamilton, London 1985).

Wacher, John, *The Towns of Roman Britain* (B.T. Batsford 1981).

Webster, Graham, *The Cornovii* (Gerald Duckworth & Co., London

1975; Allan Sutton Publishing, 1991), and *Rome Against Caractacus* (Book Club Associates, London 1981).

Westwood, Jennifer, *Albion* (Granada Publishing 1986).

Wright, Thomas, *The History of Scotland* (M'Gready, Thomson & Niven, Glasgow 18??).

INDEX

Creirwy, daughter of Clydno Eidyn
66–8, 81–2, 89, 107, 119–20, 125,
130, 148, 152
Cremthan, Irish Tribe 62, 138
Cridius, *see* Brude Grid 16
Cruithne, the 'Picts' of Ireland 7, 16,
53, 56, 141
Cruithnechan, Priest 53
Cudedda Weldig, Chief in Mannau
Gododdin 15, 40–1, 116–7, 136,
141
Culdrevney, Battle 54
Culhwch, suitor to Olwen 16
Culzean Castle and estate, 'Lordship
of Caw' 42
Cumbria or Cumberland, District 16,
20, 26, 38–9, 43, 116, 123, 127,
130, 140
Cumbric, ancient British dialect 15,
30, 77, 143
Cunedda Weldig 139–40
Cunobelinus, man of Edinburgh 120
Cunomorus, father of Drustanus 23
Custenin, son of Macsen Weldig 116
Custenin Fendigaid or Goreneu, son of
Cynfor 116
Cwm Caw(c)lwyd, Wood of Caw on
Clyde 42
Cyfarwydd, story teller 90
Cymry 10, 38, 60, 90, 138, 141, 146,
153
Cynan, King of Gwenedd 76
Cynan Garwyn 70, 120
Cynddylan, son of Llywarch Hen 106,
118–9, 152
Cyndeyrn Garthwys or St Kentigern
99
Cyndrwyn 118
Cynfarch O'Oer 9, 64, 68–9, 71, 88,
96, 98–9, 102–3, 106, 117, 120,
126, 136, 138, 140, 146
Cynfelyn or Cynvelyn 104, 120
Cynfelyn the Leprous 70

Cynfor, son of Madog 116
Cynon, *see* Kynon, son of Clydno
Eidyn

Dal Fiatach, Irish Tribe 77
Dalla, mother of Cormac 92
Dal nAraide, Clan 53
Dalriada, Scots Kingdom 3, 6, 15–17,
29, 31–2, 54–5, 57–66, 68, 71,
76–7, 80–2, 88–90, 115, 132, 135,
137–8, 144–6, 148, 150
Dalriata 60–3, 90
Dalstane 72
Damnonii or Dumnonii, British Tribe
8, 139–40, 146
Dangwyn, *see* Owain Dangwyn
Danube, River 7
Darvel, Town 85
Dawstane Rigg 72
De Excedio 44
Dega's Stone 72
Degsastan, Battle of 72
Deigr, son of Dyfnwal Hen 96
Deira, Northumbrian Kingdom 10
Delgu, Battle of 56, 65
Dementae, British Tribe 29, 42, 47, 66
Denw or Denu, daughter of Lewdwyn
Luydawc 67, 115, 130
De Situ Brecheniauc 64
Dessi, Irish Tribe 29, 62, 138
Devon 7, 20, 26, 130
Diarmit, Irish King 54
Dicaledones, British Tribe 13, 63
Dinadin, Sir 32
Dinas Eidin, Dun Eidin, Edinburgh 67,
96, 106–7, 115, 130, 140
Dingad or Dreon, son of Nudd 70
Dinguaroy or Dun Guaire, *see*
Bambro' Castle
Dinogad of Powys 70–1, 146
Dio Cassius, Historian 13
Diwrnach the Giant, owns a treasure
of Britain 6